DE...

DEAREST Birthday SHIZ BEEF —
  AKA - SHIZ
    AKA - Beef Head
    AKA - MURPHY

AKA MY SWEET 'LIL SIS &
    DEAR DEAR FRIEND...

THIS BOOK HAS BLESSED ME

TREMENDOUSLY & GREATLY HELPED
ME ON THIS HEALING
JOURNEY. I COULDN'T RESIST

SHARING THIS gift of

ENCOURAGEMENT & HOPE with
you my KINDRED spirit.

WE ALL HAVE OUR WOUNDS —
(WE JUST WON THE LOTTERY
it SEEMS) THIS IS WHERE God SHINES
BRIGHTEST... IN THE BROKEN PLACES.
So MUCH grace GIVEN TO US &
WE NOW have EVEN more to give.
HERE'S TO AN AMAZING 26th YEAR!
I Love You ♥ CASEDILLA

the wounded woman

Dr. Steve Stephens and Pam Vredevelt

Multnomah® Publishers *Sisters, Oregon*

*To all the wounded women
who refused to give up.*

THE WOUNDED WOMAN
published by Multnomah Publishers, Inc.
© 2006 by Dr. Steve Stephens and Pam Vredevelt
International Standard Book Number: 1-59052-529-9

Cover image by Pixelworks Studios, www.shootpw.com
Interior design and typeset by Katherine Lloyd, The DESK

Unless otherwise indicated, Scripture quotations are from:
The Holy Bible, New International Version © 1973, 1984 by International
Bible Society, used by permission of Zondervan Publishing House

Other Scripture quotations are from:
Holy Bible, New Living Translation (NLT) © 1996. Used by permission
of Tyndale House Publishers, Inc. All rights reserved.
New American Standard Bible® (NASB) © 1960, 1977, 1995
by the Lockman Foundation. Used by permission.
The New Testament in Modern English, Revised Edition (Phillips)
© 1958, 1960, 1972 by J. B. Phillips
The Living Bible (TLB) © 1971. Used by permission of Tyndale
House Publishers, Inc. All rights reserved.
The Holy Bible, New King James Version (NKJV) © 1984 by Thomas Nelson, Inc.
The Message © 1993, 1994, 1995, 1996, 2000, 2001, 2002
Used by permission of NavPress Publishing Group
The Amplified Bible (AMP) © 1965, 1987 by Zondervan Publishing House.
The Amplified New Testament © 1958, 1987 by the Lockman Foundation.

Multnomah is a trademark of Multnomah Publishers, Inc.,
and is registered in the U.S. Patent and Trademark Office.
The colophon is a trademark of Multnomah Publishers, Inc.

Printed in the United States of America

For information:
MULTNOMAH PUBLISHERS, INC.
601 N. LARCH STREET • SISTERS, OREGON 97759

Library of Congress Cataloging-in-Publication Data
Stephens, Steve.
The wounded woman / Steve Stephens and Pam Vredevelt.
    p. cm.
Includes bibliographical references.
ISBN 1-59052-529-9
1. Christian women--Religious life. 2. Suffering--Religious
aspects--Christianity. I. Vredevelt, Pam W., 1955- II. Title.
BV4527.S734 2006
248.8'43--dc22
                                                                                    2005025587

06 07 08 09 10—10 9 8 7 6 5 4 3 2 1 0

Contents

Acknowledgments

A special thank-you to…

Our friends Kathy Boland, Janice Eacker, Lynn Ketch, Emily Main, Barb Majors, Joy Marsh, Cari Montgomery, Kate Smith, and Marty Williams. The insights you gave after reading an early manuscript gave this book its heart and soul.

Our incredible editor, Larry Libby. You filled in the gaps and worked your magic.

Our wonderful life partners, Tami Stephens and John Vredevelt. Your support, patience, and encouragement made this book possible.

The Dark Night

[Steve]

Flowers grow out of dark moments.

Corita Kent

jenny wouldn't look at me.

She wouldn't look at anyone.

The attractive twenty-nine-year-old stared at the floor as her eyes filled with tears and her chin quivered. Curled up in the large overstuffed chair in my office, she clutched a small decorative pillow to her heart. Between sniffles she slowly told her story.

"The nights were always the scariest. That's when Daddy drank and went crazy. I never knew whether I should run away or just hide. I pulled the covers over my head and plugged my ears to drown out the yelling and cursing. I never knew what he would do once the drinking began. I was scared that he would kill Momma or me—or maybe both of us...."

For the next forty-five minutes I listened to a wounded heart spill out a story of fear and confusion, anger and guilt, sadness and hopelessness. I heard how she struggled to keep her head above the pain and how she kept being pulled beneath its surface. How she felt she was drowning and going to die. It was as if something beyond her control kept pulling her down into a dark abyss. Every once in a while she broke free, struggling to the surface, fighting for a glimpse of light and a gasp of air. But then, without warning, she found herself jerked back down into the darkness of mental anguish.

Suddenly the room was quiet.

Jenny looked up from the floor, staring at me in disbelief as I wiped a tear from my cheek. I'd been caught. I wiped away another tear and said, "It must be hard."

Her reply was barely discernable. "Thank you."

"Excuse me," I said. "What did you say?"

"Nobody has ever shed a tear for me."

The ghost of a smile touched her features, and she whispered again, *"Thank you."*

Sometimes it's impossible to maintain a detached professional objectivity when I hear people share their stories. I may feel anger over the injustices they've experienced or a sense of heavy grief over all they've suffered. There are even times when I wonder, *Oh God, why did You allow this to happen to this woman?*

We all have wounds. Some deep, some superficial. Some recent, others long ago. Some hidden, some blatantly obvious. Wounds come in myriad shapes and sizes, but they have one thing in common.

Pain.

We all deal with pain differently. Some linger too long in it—absorbed, anxious, or angry. Others try to ignore it—looking for distractions from their feelings. Still others get stuck—confused and overwhelmed by surging emotions.

In the Wake of Seven Deceptions

As we deal with wounds, the accompanying pain, and the soul-deep scars they leave behind, we want to warn you of seven misbeliefs that will make your journey to health more difficult. These beliefs bring more pain and lead to a longer journey:

1. I'm not wounded. (Denial)

2. I shouldn't talk about my wounds. (Shame)

3. My wounds reduce who I am and what I can accomplish. (Identity)

4. God did this to me. (Blame)

5. I won't seek help. (Pride)

6. Others can't help me. (Hopelessness)

7. If God cared about me, He wouldn't have let this happen. (Abandonment)

These beliefs are not healthy—and can give your wounds more power than they deserve. Wounds need not weaken or destroy you. On the contrary, they can be a life-realigning point of strength, for they force us to the inexhaustible

Source of all strength. Remember what the apostle Paul says: "God can do anything…far more than you could ever imagine or guess or request in your wildest dreams" (Ephesians 3:20, *The Message*).

We cannot change the past. What has occurred—with all its hurt, injustice, cruelty, disappointment, and tragedy—has slipped into history, beyond our control. Even so, we can change how we view the painful realities that have touched our life and what we say to ourselves about those realities.

Difficult as it may be to accept at this present moment, *you may have more control over your present situation than you think*. The prophet Jeremiah fills out the picture a little more when he writes, "'For I know the plans I have for you,' says the LORD. 'They are plans for good and not for disaster, to give you a future and a hope'" (Jeremiah 29:11, NLT).

There is great hope for every wounded woman. God heals. Pain need not last forever. Any woman, regardless of the type, severity, or impact of her wound, can have a full, peaceful—even joyful—life.

God has gentle hands. He can comfort and heal you. He can use your wounds to usher you into more meaningful and abundant days than you ever imagined possible. Jesus said, "I came that they may have life, and have it abundantly" (John 10:10, NASB). Your life might not be easy, problem free, or painless (whose is?), but it can be abundant.

Pam Vredevelt and I come to this project with over fifty years of combined experience in counseling people who have been deeply wounded by harsh realities. As you launch into this book, we want to commend you on your courage to really *do something* about your wounds. Buying and reading this book can become an important first step. And no journey can ever begin without that first step.

We also want to let you know that you are not alone. There are millions of wounded women in this world. Their circumstances and surroundings may be vastly different than yours, but pain is pain. They are your sisters, and they have stories to tell that may seem strangely familiar to you. We will tell some of these stories and explore some of the emotions behind their hurt. We realize that everybody deals with their wounds in different ways and at different paces.

So take your time reading through these chapters. Turn the pages at your own pace, absorbing the words at a rate that feels comfortable to you. Don't rush. You can read this book straight through in the order we have arranged it, or you may look at the table of contents and choose which chapters you wish to focus on first. If a particular chapter doesn't relate or is too difficult to deal with at this time, skip to the next. You may want to return to it when you are ready.

We hope and pray that this book will help you understand the healing process and give you positive tools to keep you moving forward as you work through your pain. We have written each word to remind you that there is hope and that you are not alone.

God never promised to keep us from wounds, but He did promise to be with us and to help us heal.

1. What draws you to this book—and how do you hope it will help you?

2. Which of the "Seven Misbeliefs" on page 13 have you struggled with in the past? Which ones might you currently be struggling with?

3. When have you experienced your darkest night, and what provided you a ray of hope when all felt hopeless?

4. What energizes you? Give yourself permission in the next couple of days to enjoy one hour of this favorite activity.

Too Much Rain

[Steve]

Into each life some rain must fall.

HENRY WADSWORTH LONGFELLOW

annette seemed calm.

Too calm.

She sat in my office and told me that after sixteen years of marriage, she had just discovered that her husband was having an affair.

"Have you talked to him about this?"

"Yes, and he said he was glad I found out and that it has been going on for about a year."

"So what does he want at this point?"

"To divorce me as quickly as possible and marry her," Annette replied, leaning back in her chair.

"Aren't you angry, Annette? Hurt? Depressed?"

"I suppose so," she said, "but I can't afford to waste a lot of energy on this. I've got two children to care for, and they need me to be strong."

Annette was right about one thing. Her children would

need her strength. *But burying emotions alive isn't a sign of strength.* I wanted to cry out: "Get real, woman! Your husband has brutally betrayed you. He's broken your trust. Trashed his vows. He wants to leave you and the kids. Don't pretend everything is fine. Scream! Yell! Cry! Just do something."

We all have wounds. They come with the territory on planet earth. The important issue is not whether or not we are wounded, but rather:

- Which wounds most need my attention?

- How are my wounds affecting me?

- Where am I on the path of healing?

- How can my wounds make me a stronger person?

- How can God use my wounds for good?

An old country pastor once said that there are only two types of people in the world: those who are wounded and those who are liars. Though his style was blunt and in-your-face, I believe he had a point. We all face difficult, unfair, and painful situations, and most of these leave their mark.

When we slow down and force ourselves to be honest, we often realize that all is not as it should be in our life. Certain emotions such as anger, anxiety, fear, depression, insecurity, irritability, defensiveness, confusion, negativity, melancholy, and hopelessness are potential signals trying to tell us that somewhere deep in our heart is a wound that is still tender. Some of us know exactly what sort of wound needs our attention, but some of us aren't quite sure. Wounds come in at least seven varieties.

Seven Wounds

Physical: These wounds are the most visible. In a world that places so much emphasis on outward beauty and appearance, a scar or physical impairment can be a constant reminder of an affliction due to genetics, disease, accident, or abuse. Physical wounds are painful by themselves, but more often than not they are combined with one of the following wounds, which only intensifies the hurt.

Sexual: Our sexuality is one of the most personal and vulnerable aspects of who we are. When anyone takes advantage of this part of us, deep wounds result that may affect how we see ourselves, others, and life in general. Sexual boundaries protect us, but when they are broken—whether by force, fear, or manipulation—we can feel shattered.

Choices: Sometimes we make selfish, foolish, impulsive, and poorly considered choices that leave painful marks. If we could only go back and choose differently, we would do so in a moment. But here we sit in our brokenness, with no one to blame but ourselves…which only makes the pain worse.

Verbal: Words can be as painful as any physical wound, sometimes even more so. When barbs are hurled, intentionally or unintentionally, by those we respect, trust, or lean on, the hurt can pierce us to the core. Words of discouragement, rejection, or ridicule can easily squash us, stealing our confidence and dreams.

Social: We all want to be liked. So when we feel ignored, embarrassed, excluded, marginalized, used, or attacked by others, the wound is real. Yet we frequently tell ourselves we are being immature or oversensitive, and we *shouldn't* hurt. We believe we should be able to ignore our wounds. But this really does nothing to erase the pain. How people treat us affects us—often profoundly—whether we wish to admit it or not.

Spiritual: When we feel hurt by a church, a fellow believer, the clergy, or God Himself, the wound can lead to a devastating spiritual loneliness and depression. We feel that if God or His people wound us, He must be against us or not care about us. Who can stand against God? At this point, our wounds feel like a curse, with no remedy and no hope of healing.

Emotional: Each of the above wounds carries with it an emotional component. Sometimes the original wound is so buried beneath the feelings that we can't even find it. All we are aware of is the deep, overwhelming ache and the emotions that accompany it. These emotions confuse our thinking, cloud our judgment, and too frequently block our awareness that God is beside us.

Most wounds are some combination of the above seven types, reminding us that we live in a broken world and cannot make it on our own. Wounds keep us from having a good and accurate sense of who we are and may lead us down a path of thinking too low of ourselves.

The truth is, each one of us is a package containing great potential and great limitations. The book of Genesis teaches that humankind was made in the image of God and from the dust of the earth.

Our Creator is well aware of our humble origins—and always takes them into account. David tells us that "he knows how we are formed, he remembers that we are dust" (Psalm 103:14).

Our spirit allows us to soar, but our wounds tether us to the ground. Wounds hold us back and force us to lean on the One who can truly heal all wounds.

"Listen to my cry," says the psalmist. "For my life is full of troubles" (Psalm 88:2–3, NLT). We all have our troubles, and each of these troubles creates a potential wound. Just yesterday I was speaking to a competent, attractive, thirty-four-year-old woman about how her father abandoned the family when she was six. She waved off my questions, telling me she rarely thinks about it because it's "ancient history" and "has no relevancy to my life today."

As I began asking about her father, however, tears slowly rolled down her face. She quickly wiped them away with statements like "This is stupid" or "I don't know why this bothers me."

Finally I simply said, "You stuck a bandage on the wound, but it hasn't yet healed."

"But how can that be?" She looked at me intently. "It's been *twenty-eight years*!"

"Most things fade over time," I explained, "but traumas tend to stay fresh unless treated."

Certain wounds touch the very core of who we are. It might be our personality, situation, or age that makes us more vulnerable to these wounds. It could also be the intensity, length of time, or person who wounded us that makes them so painful. Yet whatever the reason, these wounds are more traumatic than other difficulties we may have faced.

Most memories are stored in our mind chronologically. As time passes, even if the facts and images remain vivid, the intensity softens, and they have less impact on the here and now. Traumas, however, are stored *topically*. This means the pain does not fade with time. When we focus on this type of wound, regardless of whether the pain occurred long ago or yesterday, it holds the same intensity as when it first happened.

How Is Your Wound Affecting You?

The following quiz lists some symptoms that commonly occur following a wound. Understanding your hurts and how they might be affecting you is the first step to healing. You may have become so accustomed to your wound that you're hardly even aware of it. Lack of awareness, however, isn't always the same as healing. That deep hurt you've put out of your mind can still affect your life in many obvious and subtle ways.

Take a moment and read through each symptom below, marking those that you have experienced more than once in the past week. Then go back to consider what might be behind each affirmative response. Ask yourself questions like: *Are these thoughts, feelings, and behaviors normal for me, or the exception? Which of these symptoms feels the most overwhelming? How long do they last? What appears to trigger them? How disruptive are they to the flow of daily life?*

As you read through the list, be careful of the tendency to rationalize, minimize, or explain away your unhappiness. Try not to dismiss your responses with statements like "This is just the way life is" or "Everybody has their hurts" or "I could be doing a lot worse." Once finished, add up the check marks to see how deep your wounding is and how strongly it is currently affecting you. The key at the end of the quiz will help you see what you need to do next.

❑ You spontaneously become tearful for no apparent reason.

❑ You find yourself eating when you aren't hungry.

❑ You are fearful about taking risks.

❑ It is difficult to truly trust people, even yourself.

❑ At times you don't like yourself.

❑ Feelings of guilt and shame can be overwhelming.

❑ You struggle with periods of deep anger or depression.

23

- ❏ The world doesn't feel like a safe place.

- ❏ You wish you could live your life over again.

- ❏ You feel like something is wrong with you.

- ❏ You are easily startled.

- ❏ You feel lonely and detached from others.

- ❏ You do certain things to try to numb yourself from the inner pain.

- ❏ Your future doesn't seem very positive.

- ❏ It's hard to let go of the past.

- ❏ You're always expecting something bad to happen.

- ❏ Life doesn't seem very fair.

- ❏ Nightmares, flashbacks, or emotional flooding can leave you upset for days.

- ❏ Feeling safe and protected is very important to you.

- ❏ It's hard for you to fully relax.

If you checked…	Your wounds are probably…
1–6	Mild to moderate—be careful
7–12	Serious—you need to do something
13–20	Severe—get help now!

There Is Always Hope

Wounds are a part of reality, and reality frequently offers large portions of hurt and harshness. When I was at one of

the lowest points of my life, I remember crying out
but feeling like there was no response. More accurately, the
pain was so consuming that I could neither see nor hear the
God I wanted so much to lean upon.

It was at that point that I turned to wise and godly
counsel. Surely, they could give me hope. They told me to
pray more and read Scripture more and trust God more.

These are good things.

Every one of them.

But they did nothing to ease my pain.

Instead, their answers felt like salt and sand rubbed
deeper into the wound. My "counselors" gave me formulas.
But nobody *listened*, nobody came close, nobody cried.
They gave their quick fix and kept their distance. I shook
my head and walked away, feeling alone and abandoned.

Out of this situation I became determined to understand how to relate to people in pain. I wanted to learn how
to give compassion and comfort. In Jeremiah's darkest hour
he heard God say, "I will give you back your health and heal
your wounds" (30:17, NLT). This is the promise we all yearn
for when we feel the most desperate and hopeless. King
David wept as he wrote, "My heart is wounded within me"
(Psalm 109:22).

Hannah Whitall Smith, one of the bestselling Christian
writers of all time, went through periods of deep discouragement and despair. Four of her seven children died before
adulthood. One daughter left her husband for an artist and
another daughter left her faith to marry atheist Bertrand

25

Russell. Her husband was an international evangelist who had several nervous breakdowns and several affairs, which led to a public scandal. Friends abandoned her, and arthritis shadowed her days with great physical pain. Yet through it all she held on to her faith, writing books like *The Christian's Secret of a Happy Life* and *The God of All Comfort.*

At one point of overwhelming stress and pain, she wrote, "See God in everything, and God will calm and color all that thou dost see." In the midst of your wounds we wish to help you not only see God, but also feel His strong, gentle arms holding you…comforting you…supporting you…and never letting you go.

1. What did you identify with in the list of wounds on pages 19–20?

2. How do these struggles make your day-to-day life more of a challenge?

3. Within your circle of acquaintance, who do you know who has experienced painful wounds? Have they been able to move forward? What helped them the most?

4. Take thirty minutes in the next few days to sit outside and inhale deep breaths of fresh air. Note the sounds and smells around you.

Lampposts in the Dark

[Pam]

> I can stand what I know.
> It is what I don't know that frightens me.
>
> FRANCES NEWTON

n my counseling office and during my travels as a speaker, I frequently hear women ask questions like these:

- ❁ How can I let go of the pain?

- ❁ Will I ever get beyond the heartache?

- ❁ How much time does it take to heal?

- ❁ What should I expect in the days ahead?

These women genuinely long for rock-solid answers in the midst of the harsh realities of their lives. They want to know how to manage their pain and what to expect during their "dark night of the soul." A little bit of knowledge can bring reassurance like a bright light on a dark and unknown path, revealing what the night hides.

When we suffer a psychological wound, the mind begins a process of recuperation every bit as natural as the healing of a physical wound. However, while physical injuries can heal fairly quickly with the help of modern medicine, the pain of a wounded heart can linger for years and is far more stubborn, elusive, and challenging to identify.

Processing pain can be downright confusing. Sadness, powerlessness, ambivalence, anger, agitation, and confusion can unpredictably flood us. Although these feelings are often frightening and difficult to understand, they aren't wrong. In fact, they are normal responses and necessary for us to grow.

In fact, feeling is an integral part of healing.

Feeling Is Healing

Feeling leads to release. Denying, stuffing, or numbing our feelings with some sort of addictive behavior only prolongs and intensifies our pain. It blocks us from moving forward. Repressing our feelings may give us a sense of protection, but it requires a tremendous amount of energy. It's like trying to keep a beach ball underwater when all it wants to do is force its way to the surface. Allowing feelings to come to the surface can bring healing and provide us with the extra energy we need to rebuild our life.

I remember the ache in my empty arms after our first baby died halfway to term. With postpartum hormones raging, the grief was more than I wanted to endure. I said to one of my colleagues at the counseling center where I worked, "I wish there were a pill I could take that would make these feelings go away."

He was very kind and, like a good friend, spoke the truth in love: "I can sure understand that, but then you would just have to work through your grief later."

He was making a point I understand more fully now. Healing demands that we feel and ride out our painful emotions. When we are feeling our pain, we are progressing. We tend to get mixed up about this. We think that if we feel deeply, we're losing it, cracking up, or having a mental breakdown. This simply isn't true!

One of the statements I frequently share with wounded women is: *Fish swim, birds fly, people feel. Feeling is healing.*

We must give ourselves and others permission to feel. While we are allowing our feelings to surface and purging the pain from our heart, it can also be helpful to know some of the reference points or mile markers on the road of recovery. When we embark on a journey, it's nice to have a general idea of what lies ahead. Experiences that meet our expectations are easier to handle, even if they are extremely painful. When we know what to expect, we can more easily adjust.

Relief comes from knowing we are headed in the right direction, even when we know we have a long way to go.

I shared some of these reference points recently with Sheri, a young woman suffering terrible anguish after being raped. Her life was in shambles. She couldn't get out of bed in the morning. Convinced she was damaged goods, she thought that her crying, confusion, and fears of going crazy would never end. The emotional roller coaster led her into a pattern of compulsive eating. Her physical and emotional wounds had immobilized her. Fortunately, Sheri's best friend knew that she needed help and encouraged her to meet with me. After listening to Sheri's heartbreaking story, I offered a few thoughts about what she might experience in the months ahead.

"Sheri, you have been wounded physically and psychologically. Your physical wounds will heal much faster than your heart wounds. But in time, you will heal. As you are healing, you will likely pass through three phases: Crisis, Recoil, and Reorganization.

"You're in the Crisis Phase right now. Your nerves are raw. It's hard to concentrate. It seems like your mind is short-circuiting because the horror of what you've been through has overloaded your mental computer. The good news is, this phase won't last forever. It's temporary, and your best friend and I will help you get through it. You won't have to do this alone. Things will likely feel worse before they feel better, but you will heal, and a year from now you'll be in a very different place...."

I didn't want to overwhelm Sheri with too much information, so before she left I handed her a list of reference points on the road of recovery, hoping they would serve as lampposts in the dark.

Lampposts in the Dark

The Crisis Phase:

Marked by intense emotion, this phase begins when we first suffer a wound. We may feel flooded with sadness, anger, rage, confusion, and anxiety. We try to make decisions, but it's as though our gears are locked and we can't move. Thoughts seem scrambled. Nerves are raw, with an over-whelming sense that *This is more than I can bear!* Feelings of hopelessness and helplessness seem all-consuming.

Some may go into shock and on the outside appear as if nothing happened. Emotions are buried alive and blocked from consciousness. Flashbacks of the incident or obsessive replays of the wound rob us of clear thinking during the day, and nightmares steal peaceful sleep. This phase typically lasts from a few days to a few months, depending on the magnitude of the wound and the support and resources available to us. When we resume a fairly regular routine, even if it feels like we're just going through the motions, we pass out of the Crisis Phase into the Recoil Phase.

The Recoil Phase:

During this phase we try our best to get back to life as it was before the wound. Things seem to be getting better. We have settled down and now begin to face the facts and feel the feelings related to our wound. Difficult emotions such as anger, rage, guilt, fear, anxiety, sadness, despair, and

33

powerlessness surface. Not all of these feelings can be confronted at the same time. But they can be confronted little by little. Healing comes in bits and pieces, slowly but surely.

In this phase we flip-flop between denial and resolution. Some days we have the internal strength to think about the wound and to talk about it with God and safe friends. Other days, we have to put the ordeal on the back burner and say, "I'm going to leave it alone today and give my mind a rest from it all." Both approaches are valid and helpful.

The Reorganization Phase:

In this phase we focus less on our wound and the pain of the past and more on the present and future. We focus forward on the road ahead and glance less frequently in the rearview mirror. Pain no longer dominates our days or drives our choices. We are calmer. The sadness, fear, anger, guilt, and shame that once seemed to overwhelm us may still be present, but are no longer as frequent or intense. Though waves of pain wash back over us from time to time, we are able to acknowledge them, feel them, and let them go. Our heartache doesn't linger as long or run as deep. We find our concentration improved, our energy returning, and our ability to make decisions nearly back on track.

Our pain begins to take its proper place as we come to experience our wound as one thin slice of the big pie of life.

That's so important. *Our wound is not the whole pie.* It certainly felt that way in the Crisis Phase, but now we are able to acknowledge and accept it as one part of our total life experience. With the passing of time, we learn how to integrate it with other aspects of life.

Peace and healing come in the context of relationships.

Mental anguish is an invisible wound that often goes unnoticed by others. As a result many women suffer alone, and their healing is delayed. When you are healing, it is critical that you risk in relationships. *Fight* the inner voice that says, "Don't talk about it; don't bother them with the details," and reach out. As you allow safe people to help you bear your burden by authentically sharing your thoughts and feelings, your healing will be accelerated. The opposite is also true. Isolation can retard growth and healing.

It's natural to pull back from everyone and everything when we've suffered a wound, much as we would yank our finger away from a flame to protect ourselves from more burns. But if we remain recoiled and detached—closing God and others out of our suffering—we will derail our own healing.

As I think over my own life and the times of deep sadness and overwhelming grief, I can see that my greatest moments of relief came when I sensed that God or a trusted friend was truly present with me in my pain. It was as if someone opened the door on my darkness, walked in, sat down with me, and, with full acceptance, waited.

My wound was our meeting place.

Inner peace and healing were born within that connection.

Their companionship in my suffering brought relief, even though the circumstances evoking the pain remained the same.

I don't know why we have such difficulty asking for emotional support when we need it. Why is it that we will see a medical doctor for a broken bone much faster than we'll seek assistance for a broken heart? I'm told that a broken bone may eventually get better, even if left untreated, but it may not function very well. The same thing can happen when we leave the invisible wounds in our soul unattended.

Yes, the memory of the wound may diminish over time. But if it doesn't truly *heal*, we may end up hindered in the ways we relate to others. Instead of escaping our pain, we'll be in danger of re-creating it again and again.

Here's the good news: When we face the facts of our wound and bring our thoughts to and share our heart with God and safe friends, healing happens. It may not come as quickly as we want, or as easily as we want, but it does come. Many women find themselves in the Recoil Phase for a year or more, depending on the gravity of their wound, the strength of their relationship with God, and the availability of good support. When we face and embrace our pain with God and the others who support us, eventually we find ourselves in phase three of the healing journey.

When you've been wounded, find safe friends who...
Don't shock easily, but accept your feelings.
Don't give unwanted advice.
Help you recall your strengths.
Trust you to be able to come through this difficult time.
Treat you like an adult who can make your own decisions.

Respect your courage and sense of determination.
Understand that grief is normal.
Have been through difficult times and can share their
*   experiences with you.*
Try to understand what your feelings mean to you.
Pray with you and for you.

Putting Pain in Perspective

Perspective comes as we pay attention to what we say to ourselves about our wound. It's important that we don't "catastrophize" our pain by saying, "I can't handle this! This is the worst thing that could ever happen to me…. I can't bear to go on…."

It doesn't help to slip into doomsday fortune-telling: "The rest of my life is ruined…. There is no possible way I can go on…. The future is hopeless…."

Never mind the fact that these statements are false. All-or-nothing thinking can also block us from forward movement. We want to avoid saying things to ourselves like: "Nobody cares what I'm going through. Everything in my life is going wrong. Life will always be this hard. Nothing will ever change."

When we are emotionally fragile, we can easily blame ourselves for things that were completely beyond our control. When Sheri told me her story of being assaulted, I learned that her offender was a guy from school who asked her out on a date. As she tried to make sense of the shocking horror, her mind kept searching for things she might have done to cause the rape.

Part of Sheri's healing came from realizing that she had done *nothing* to cause this. Her offender chose to do what he did, and she had been unable to control his vicious behavior. She did the best she could to defend herself at the time, but he was bigger and stronger and mercilessly threatened her life. She was simply no match for his formidable force.

It took courage—more courage than she thought she had—but Sheri spent several months in counseling where she acknowledged, revisited, and processed her trauma. Facing the truth about her losses and how they affected her life gradually defused the power of her pain. Each week I saw change. At first tears and, eventually, spontaneous smiles broke through the barrier of Sheri's cold stares. Bit by bit, stone by stone, she dismantled the wall she had built around her heart and risked letting the pain out and others in.

In time, Sheri gained the courage to join a support group for other wounded women in recovery. One night the group wanted to talk about "God issues" and how they perceived God's involvement in their lives. The group leader passed out paper and markers, asking each member to draw a picture illustrating her relationship with God.

One woman drew a stick figure of herself—no face, no hair, no clothes—kneeling on one side of a stone wall that towered high above her. Her face was buried in her hands. Bright sunlight shone on the other side of the wall, where Jesus stood with scores of other stick figures. She described herself as someone on the outside looking in. "I feel as if God has all kinds of friends down here on earth," she said, "but I'm not one of them."

As we went around the circle, each woman showed the others her picture. When it was Sheri's turn, she held up a likeness of two very large hands holding the handles of an ornate vase. There were many colored markers she could have used, but she chose to do her picture strictly in black. The outline of the vase was carefully drawn and perfectly symmetrical. But down the middle of the vase she had drawn a thick, jagged line depicting a very deep crack. Her description moved me.

"It can't be fixed," she said slowly. "The hands holding it are about to throw it away."

It wasn't a pretty picture, but even so, Sheri took a step forward that night. She was open with others about how she felt concerning her relationship with God.

One of the other members, Terry, immediately stepped in and asked Sheri *how* the vase had become cracked. Terry, herself a rape victim, happened to be nearing the end of her recovery. Within the safety of the group, Sheri was able to uncover the shame-filled events of her date rape. It was incredible to see God do a deep work in Sheri through those women who offered her acceptance, grace, and truth.

Sheri's bitterness began to change in subtle ways. It didn't happen fast, but then long-term change rarely does. As the months passed, her eating problems became less and less of an issue. Why? Because the pain driving her compulsion was losing its power. Sheri was learning to face her pain and let it go, so there was less need for food to be an anesthetic.

One day Sheri walked into my office and said, "I've made a decision. I want to be trained to work on the rape crisis hotline." She didn't want others to suffer in silence or live in denial, as she had for so many years. She wanted to be a refuge for those who were scared and hiding. She wanted God to use her brokenness to help others heal.

Toward the end of Sheri's recovery, the group again raised "God issues." Each of the women received a clean sheet of paper and colored markers, and when they were finished, they showed the others their new drawings.

Sheri's new picture intrigued me. Once again she drew a perfectly symmetrical vase with swirly handles on the sides. Once again, the same two large hands firmly gripped it. The deep crack down the middle of the vase was still there, too.

But Sheri had added something new. Using a fluorescent yellow marker, she had drawn heavy lines, like beams of light, spilling out of the fissure and flowing to the edge of the paper. Pointing to the crack, she said, "*That's* where God shines through."

Once again I was reminded that it is through our suffering, our trials, and our wounds that God's glory is often revealed. The caption under Sheri's picture could have read "2 Corinthians 4":

For God, who said, "Let light shine out of darkness," made his light shine in our hearts to give us the light of the knowledge of the glory of God in the face of Christ. But we have this treasure in jars of clay to show that this all-surpassing power is from God and not from us. We are hard pressed on every side, but not crushed; perplexed, but not in despair; persecuted, but not abandoned; struck down, but not destroyed. (vv. 6–9)

Unadorned clay pots. Vases with cracks. Earthenware jars with chips and dings and flaws. People with troubles, perplexities, weaknesses, traumas, and fears. That's all we are without God.

But *with* God...oh, we are so much more.

With God, we are people with a treasure inside, a treasure whose value is beyond price, reckoning, or comprehension. We are women with God's glory at work in us. His work doesn't entail removing our weaknesses or hardships. No, His work is displayed as He releases His divine power *through* our weaknesses.

When life is hard and God is in us, our broken places can become the windows where His glory shines through.

When life is hard and God is in us, we who are broken pots can become trophies.

When life is hard and God is in us, we can rest assured that somehow, in some way, He will bring His redeeming glory to bear in our life and in the lives of others.

The longer I work with wounded women, the more I am convinced that if a heart is open and truthful, there is *no* pain so deep or pervasive that God cannot heal it. Those who have been wounded and healed are then gifted in helping others heal. Wounds change us. They call forth our courage. They demand that we grow mentally, emotionally, and spiritually. When we face and embrace our pain, we are never again the same. We are better.

And as with Sheri, the broken places of our life—the fractures, fissures, and jagged edges—can become the very locales where God's glory spills through in a torrent of light, hope, and healing. Out of our own personal darkness, God's penetrating light can touch those who still grope in the shadows.

Just ask one of the regulars on the rape crisis hotline.

1. Scribble down all the feelings you have experienced in the last week on one piece of paper. Circle the three feelings that have been most overwhelming.

2. Which of the following phases are you currently experiencing?

   Crisis: intense confusion and emotion

   Recoil: things seem to be settling down and getting better

   Reorganization: you're moving forward

3. Refer to the "Characteristics of Safe People" on pages 36–37. Make a point of reaching out to at least one safe person this week.

4. Write a poem, paint a picture, or create a magazine collage that captures the feelings of your heart.

Good Grief

[Pam]

Grief only comes in one size...extra large.

DENNIS MANNING

put her letter down, wiped the tears from my cheeks, and wondered if I had the strength to read on. Her opening sentences stole my breath away: "It has been a very hard year for us. Our son took his life in April."

"No!" I cried in disbelief. "This can't be happening to Mike and Susie. Not them!"

Their letter revealed more of the story:

Cleaning out Jon's apartment, we found diaries from his college years. He had great plans. Impressive plans. But he was the victim of a mental illness that strikes young adults in their prime, paranoid schizophrenia. His fears of imaginary plots against him, and CIA surveillance, along with never ending voices taunting him as a failure immobilized him. For eight long years he tried, but could not defeat the unrelenting voices. In his mind, there was only one way out. In defiance against his tormentors, he ended his life.

Jon's descent into his darkness began his last year of college. As parents we felt utterly helpless. Parents want to rescue, to fix, to solve the problems of their children. We tried, but nothing helped as we watched his condition get worse. No vocabulary is adequate to describe the insurmountable pain of these last few years, and our present pain. Children are not supposed to die before their parents....

There are a lot of things that aren't "supposed" to happen. Vicious homicides. Terrible accidents. Traumatic births. Handicaps. Terminal illnesses. Untimely transfers. Pink slips. Bankruptcies. Divorce. Death. These losses leave gaping wounds. Those suffering in their wake either get better or worse. None stay the same.

As I write this chapter I think of several friends who are agonizing over significant losses. Mike and Susie grieve for their son, Jon. Sandy and Rob mourn their dearly loved sister whose life was snuffed out by a drunk driver crossing the centerline at sixty miles-an-hour. Terry and Bill struggle to keep their own heads up, while helping their son bear the never-ending burden of a serious mental illness.

Their grief lingers. It leaves these very capable and competent people feeling as if they're running on fumes. In the darkest moments of despair they secretly wonder:

"What's the point of going on?" Sorrow won't leave them alone, *and the greater the loss, the greater the pain.*

Is sorrow an uninvited guest in your life? Do you find yourself groping in the shadows of painful memories and wounds you prefer not to think about? If so, you have likely realized that grief is *not* a path to travel alone. It's too oppressive. Too confusing. Too scary. You need someone to help you see your way through the gloom.

I can offer you a map.

Your friends and family can offer you support.

But God is the One who knows all the details and is best equipped to lead you along this foreign path into brighter new beginnings. Self-reliance will mislead you. God won't. He makes this promise:

> "I will lead the blind by ways they have not known,
> along unfamiliar paths I will guide them; I will turn
> the darkness into light before them and make the
> rough places smooth. These are the things I will do;
> I will not forsake them." (Isaiah 42:16)

I don't know the way through your darkness. Only God does. Yes, I have suffered grief in ways that are familiar to some, but everyone's grief experience is different. Your wounds are unique to you. Your healing process will also be one of a kind.

Please pay close attention. I want you to grab on tight to what I'm am going to say next. It is our bottom-line assumption about grief. Your pain is not a problem. It is a solution.

The grief you have experienced—or still endure—is a driving force. The emotional energy generated by that grief is what will press you to examine yourself, your worldview, and your beliefs in God, and eventually enable you to adjust to your loss. It is what will energize you to change, adapt, grow, and move through the valley of the shadows and out the other side, back into the sunlight.

Grief isn't the road *to* healing.

Grief is the road *of* healing.

And it is familiar territory for Jesus.

Isaiah says of our suffering Savior: "He was despised and rejected—a man of sorrows, acquainted with bitterest grief" (Isaiah 53:3, NLT). The book of Hebrews reminds us that as our great High Priest, Jesus is never "out of touch with our reality. He's been through weakness and testing, experienced it all—all but the sin. So let's walk right up to him and get what he is so ready to give. Take the mercy, accept the help" (4:15–16, *The Message*).

He is fully aware of your bitter heartache and knows the way through your suffering. The operative word is *through*. You won't feel desperate forever. You have God's guarantee on this: "'But I will restore you to health and heal your wounds,' declares the LORD" (Jeremiah 30:17).

This may be difficult for you to accept right now, but it is perfectly true: *Desperation is productive if it drives us to God.* It presents us with opportunities to watch God display

His grace and power in our life. It gives us a chance to just stand back a little and witness God doing what man cannot do. It allows us to experience God becoming whatever we need Him to be as He escorts us along the path of healing. We come to know Him as our God of Comfort. Our Strength. Our Shield. Our Security. Our Safe Place. Our Peace.

Growing out of the aftermath of deep wounds can be a scary, steep, and rocky road. Tough terrain. Sharp cliffs. Unpredictable turns. Darkness blinds us from being able to see beyond the end of our nose. The journey down this road includes very intense internal reactions: denial, anxiety, guilt, sorrow, and anger. The sum total of these reactions is what we call grief.

Grief is not logical.

Grief is not linear.

There is nothing neat and tidy or orderly about this process. If someone tries to apply a 1-2-3 formula to where you are in life right now, they're not doing you any favors (and really don't know what they're talking about). Grief is chock-full of irrational, turbulent, confusing, and unpredictable cycles of emotion. It is jam-packed with troubling, intrusive thoughts that don't pass through our mind when we are experiencing brighter days.

Our temper is short.

We feel guilty over little things.

We second-guess ourselves.

We love and hate at the same time.

We want to be alone and yet crave close connections.

We can move from resigned hopelessness to bold defiance in a single heartbeat.

Grief is a time of massive contradictions. In my own personal experience, and for many others I've known, grief has been nothing even close to a clean, step-by-step process. On the contrary, the sorrow that grips our life is very confusing, and feelings typically race in and out without any logical progression. Emotions are mixed, seemingly random. In most cases they boil to the surface repeatedly—and more frequently than we prefer.

God has wired us so that our pain serves a purpose. It can tell us important information about our values, our beliefs, and ourselves if we take time to tune in and listen. Our feelings are a gift from God to propel us forward in the healing process. There really isn't a strict order to the process, but something like a loose pattern of reactions can often be observed. Denial always pops up first, but it reappears over and over again whenever we sense our pain pushing us too close to the cliff edge of despair.

The Gift of Denial

We typically respond to major disappointment and loss with a defense mechanism called denial. This was my immediate response to Susie's letter. Upon reading the news about her precious son, I instantly said, "No! This can't be happening!" All of my defenses went up.

Denial is one of the abilities God has given us to help us buy time in order to find the inner strength and external resources we need to cope. It allows us to not have to deal with our painful reality all at once. It is a gift that can ease us through the mind-assaulting separation from whomever or whatever we have lost. It helps us pace ourselves so we can manage our heartache a little at a time.

We release denial's hold over our mind when we face the truth. As awareness of our loss increases, so does our pain. Facing the facts can be extremely difficult. We ping-pong back and forth between seeing reality for what it is and shutting it out altogether.

I remember experiencing this flip-flop between facing reality and denial after our sixteen-year-old daughter's car was rear-ended by an eighteen-wheel semi on the freeway. My mind simply wasn't able to embrace all the facts at once.

I'll never forget the evening my husband and I sat with the doctor as he explained our daughter's tests results following her accident. My mind kept checking in and out of our conversation. I heard the doctor say one thing, and then I heard myself say, *I don't believe this is happening.*

That's how denial can work for us. It protects us from being fire-hosed by the bitter truth and allows us to take small, manageable sips as we are able. In fact, *a little bit of denial is good for what ails you.*

Too much of a good thing, however, is not good a thing at all. Ongoing denial can arrest the grief process and trap people in their pain. I remember Lori, a forty-six-year-old woman who told me about Matthew, the baby she had lost fourteen years earlier in stillbirth.

"It's over," her family told her. "Forget it. Don't talk about it. We have to move on." And that's exactly what she did. She moved on, stayed busy, got involved in things, and kept her mind occupied.

Oh yes, she moved on.

But not really.

Lori didn't move on emotionally.

Her heart was tightly wedged in an incident long past. She was frozen in time, arrested in grief.

Matthew's name had not been mentioned since the day Lori left the hospital. There was no funeral, no memorial, no pictures, no discussion. Lori and her family treated the incident as if it had never happened. Cards sent by friends were burned unopened. The family thought that erasing the evidence would erase the pain.

But it didn't. It couldn't.

So now there were fourteen years of repressed, stockpiled pain. This was the way Lori handled other losses, too. No wonder she was depressed. No wonder she felt as if she were about to burst. *The human heart was never designed to bury feelings alive.*

When Lori came to see me, she found the courage to recognize and face reality for the first time in fourteen years. Behind closed doors she gave herself permission to recognize her loss and talk about it—an oh-so-important step in her healing. The denial was broken, and so was the power of the pain. As Margaret Lee Runbeck wrote, "There is no power on earth more formidable than the truth."

Anxiety

When we suffer loss, change is forced upon us, and we have no say in the matter. Nothing stays the same. The dreams we once had are shattered, and somehow we have to find a way to go on.

Hearing the news that our son had Down syndrome and heart problems forced John and me to dramatically alter our lives. The dreams we had envisioned for our future vanished like a puff of mist. Changing our lifestyle and changing our dreams weren't easy for us. When these changes are imposed on us rather than chosen, the natural response is anxiety.

Even anxiety, however, serves a positive purpose. It drives us to take action.

The anxiety I experienced after Nathan's catastrophic birth energized me to take a leave of absence and then to eventually resign from a job. While these were difficult changes, they proved healthy and necessary for the stabilization of our family. Our anxiety related to Nathan's heart problems drove us to seek prayer support, to research our options, and to secure the best medical care possible. When we felt as if we were running on fumes, anxiety pushed us to take action.

Anxiety acts like a smoke alarm. It warns us that something serious needs our attention. It alerts us that things beyond our control are happening. However, when anxiety is triggered quickly by a sense of abandonment, we may wrongly conclude, "People or God have left me all alone."

Whether the abandonment is real or perceived is irrelevant. The anxiety response is the same. Anxiety is also triggered by the extreme sense of vulnerability that surfaces following a loss. We didn't ask for this loss, but we got it anyway. We find ourselves assailed by the thought, "If I didn't have a say in this, will I have a say in anything?"

Even though anxiety is an unpleasant feeling, it too can be a driving force in the healing process. It presses us to face the awful reality of our wounds and lost dreams. The anxiety of being alone in our struggle energizes us to reach out when isolation seems easier. We risk attaching to new people and new dreams because to not do so is even scarier. The fear of feeling *this* fragile for the rest of our life forces us to ask tough questions and seek God. It drives us to search for meaning, purpose, new direction, and resolution. In this sense, anxiety is not bad; it is functional.

But as with denial, too much of something can become problematic. In a later chapter, we will suggest ways to keep your anxiety in check so that it works for you rather than against you.

HOW TO HELP ME AS I GRIEVE

Don't avoid me.

Understand that I need to be alone sometimes.

Please don't give advice.

Don't take over for me. I need to do some things for myself.

Give me time. Don't expect too much too soon.

Remember my loved one with me.

Don't try to fix me.

Accept my silence. Listen to my story.

Guilt

Not long after Nathan's birth, the following conversation took place at the athletic club during John's regular workout.

"So…did you have the baby yet?"

"Yes." John nodded, in no mood to talk.

"Great! So is it a boy or a girl?"

"It's a boy."

The man must have noticed that John wasn't his typical jovial self, because his next question was:

"So…is something wrong?"

"Yes. He has Down syndrome and heart problems."

"Well…did you have any tests done before he was born?"

"No. There was no indication that anything was wrong."

Shaking his head with a scowl, he retorted, "Certainly something could have been done to prevent this…." Moving on with his routine, he reached for another set of dumbbells. End of conversation.

The judgment rang out loud and clear: "You shouldn't have allowed this to happen. There must have been something you could have done to prevent it." The man had just thrown a hand grenade at an already-wounded dad and then went on with his routine as though nothing had happened.

It's easy to tell ourselves the same kind of messages when we've been wounded. We hold ourselves responsible, convinced that in some way what we are suffering is our own fault. We must have done something to cause this.

In our efforts to make sense of our wounds, we may erroneously conclude that God is punishing us for past or present wrongs. If we have gone through life believing that God blesses good people with good things, and then something bad happens to us, we surmise we must be bad. Pinning the blame on something, even if it is ourselves, seems to increase our sense of control. This, however, is faulty thinking, and reflects our feeble attempts to understand and explain what cannot be explained this side of heaven.

When we suffer loss, everything we have ever believed about our ability to influence life and control our destiny gets challenged. Our nice, neat categories of right and wrong and cause and effect get scrambled. What's the point of living a moral, ethical, law-abiding life if the man driving the semi that plowed into my daughter lies through his teeth to avoid paying for damages? Our sense of justice rises from within screaming, "This is not right!" It's human nature to want to reestablish order and to pin the blame somewhere.

I like to think of guilt as a red flag. It can be a cue to examine what you are saying to yourself about the cause of your wound and the responsibility you feel over what has happened.

If the wounding you've suffered was beyond your control, then you have no responsibility. Any false guilt you're packing around is unnecessary suffering.

Let it go.

False guilt will do nothing but sap emotional energy needed for healing and arrest your forward movement. Understand that when you try to take responsibility for something that was beyond your control, you are simply making a misguided attempt to reestablish a sense of control in your life. Later we will offer several specific tools that can prevent you from booking reservations on guilt trips. For now, let's consider guilt as a feeling that can drive us to explore our views on cause and effect.

Guilt is also a healthy emotion that can lead us to bow our knees and humbly receive God's forgiveness. Christ's passion to pardon our guilt led Him to lay down His life:

> It was our weaknesses he carried; it was our sorrows that weighed him down. And we thought his troubles were a punishment from God for his own sins! But he was wounded and crushed for our sins. He was beaten that we might have peace. He was whipped, and we were healed! All of us have strayed away like sheep. We have left God's paths to follow our own.

Yet the LORD laid on him the guilt and sins of us all. (Isaiah 53:4–6, NLT)

If Jesus were to meet with you face-to-face in the safety of your living room, He would do everything possible to reassure you. I imagine Him saying something like: "I know about all of those things you've never mentioned to a soul. I was there when you made those mistakes...and I took the punishment for you. I'm fully aware of your poor decisions, and I've already paid the penalty. Your debt has been canceled. I suffered and died so you wouldn't have to bear the burden of your shame. Lay your bags of guilt at the foot of My cross. I have already forgiven you. Learn from what went wrong, and move on. Allow My wounds to serve their purpose. Receive My gift of forgiveness. Entrust your heart to Me. I will carefully mend it piece by piece...."

Nothing we have ever done has caught God by surprise. He sees all and knows all. And with a full awareness of our faults and failures, He declares His commitment to love us to health: "I have seen what [you] do, but I will heal [you] anyway! I will lead [you] and comfort those who mourn" (Isaiah 57:18, NLT).

God knows us better than we know ourselves. He can identify our deepest needs and address them in ways that cut through all the turmoil and transform us.

Shortly after Nathan was born I remember trying to sort through my confusion about the causes of his Down syndrome. I felt guilty for being so sad. I felt guilty for feeling anxious about what the future might hold.

I turned to a friend of mine whose twelve-year-old daughter was also handicapped. Wise lady that she is, Kay didn't give me any simple platitudes or pat answers. Instead, she pointed me back to Scripture. She told me that one of the passages that had been meaningful to their family since Kara's birth was John chapter 9. Eager for answers, I immediately picked up my Bible and began to read:

> Walking down the street, Jesus saw a man blind from birth. His disciples asked, "Rabbi, who sinned: this man or his parents, causing him to be born blind?"
>
> Jesus said, "You're asking the wrong question. You're looking for someone to blame. There is no such cause-effect here. Look instead for what God can do." (John 9:1–3, *The Message*)

God spoke to me through those verses and challenged me to quit trying to "figure it all out." I was wasting my energy looking for a cause. I was asking the wrong questions. Instead, He wanted me to shift my focus. He wanted me to intentionally look for what *He* could do. He wanted me to experience His power and provision, His tenderness and care. It was fresh perspective that removed some of the gloom, enabling me to see a bit more clearly. The shadows began to lose their tenacious grip.

Sorrow

"I feel like I'm standing at the bottom of the Grand Canyon surrounded by towering walls of stone," Susan told me. "I have no idea how to find my way out of here, but at least I'm standing on solid rock."

Susan is a vibrant young woman who lost her husband the week before Christmas. He was thirty-three. Married seven years, they had been expecting their first child.

Six months later sorrow is still Susan's closest companion. Everything in their home reminds her of Tim. Not an hour passes that she doesn't think of the times they had together or of the dreams they shared for their future. She wonders if the tears will ever stop and has moments when she can't bear to go on.

Deep sorrow can be terrifying.

Grieving parents tell me they feel like they are losing their minds. I recall moments in my own grief when I wondered if something was seriously wrong with me because I couldn't climb out of a seemingly bottomless black hole. I knew others who were suffering extreme losses, and they appeared to be "coping better." What was my hang-up? Why was it taking so long for me to bounce back?

Sorrow talks. Have you heard its voice?

It says to the wounded, "Get real. Things are *not* going to get better. You're marred for life. Nothing will ever change. Whatever you do really doesn't matter. The good days are gone—gone forever." As we grope our way through the dark, grief convinces us that we are helpless and hopeless.

But that's sorrow talking.

That's the voice of emotions over the edge.

It's not truth.

The *truth* is, God is with us, and He is anything but passive on our behalf. On the contrary, He works actively for our highest good. He is intentional. His direction is strategic. He moves behind the scenes, orchestrating details and events in ways that cannot be perceived by the human eye. He's shaping. He's creating. We are being changed, reconstructed, restored. He is ordering our steps and leading us through the dark. Eventually the heavy gray clouds will lift, and we'll see things more clearly. Just as surely as grief comes, it goes.

In the meantime, there are lessons to be learned in the dark. There are treasures to be discovered. If we avoid pain or seek escape routes around the valley of sorrow, we will be the poorer for it, forfeiting incredible riches that are part of the heavenly game plan. God says, "I will give you treasures hidden in the darkness—secret riches. I will do this so you may know that I am the LORD…the one who calls you by name" (Isaiah 45:3, NLT).

Hidden treasures…secret riches…wreathed in darkness.

Some of the greatest, richest discoveries of my life have come during times of crushing sorrow. The riches were not material. They were spiritual. Treasures of another dimension. In the darkest nights He graced me with eyes of faith, night vision that enabled me to see and understand that which had never been perceptible to me before. He revealed areas of my life that needed to change, all the while reassuring me that He would supply whatever resources I needed.

I recall a night about six months after Jessie's accident when she was very sick with dizziness, nausea, and a splitting headache. I was weary from the sorrow of watching her suffer through these bouts month after month with little change. She was in her junior year of high school, and I was riddled with "what-ifs."

What if she doesn't get better? What if no one can help her? What if she can't graduate?

My head spun round and round with worst-case scenarios. I crawled into bed that night and cried myself to sleep.

Around 3:00 a.m. I woke up. Strangely, my first waking thought was of a dream I'd had the summer before she entered high school. *How odd.* I usually don't remember my dreams, but this one was different. In fact, it was so vivid I sat up and wrote it in my journal.

In the dream I saw Jessie standing in a cap and gown on the stage at high school graduation. She seemed happy and was saying something to the audience. What I heard in my heart puzzled me: *"She will be fine. It will be a fight, and I will do the fighting for you."*

The words were familiar. I had memorized them years before when studying the life of Moses. The nation of Israel was on its mass Exodus out of Egypt and everything seemed to be going wrong. With the Red Sea before them and Egyptian warriors quickly closing in from behind, the Israelites cried out to God in panicked desperation. From higher ground, Moses hushed the crowd and boldly declared: "Don't be afraid. Just stand where you are and watch the LORD rescue you....The LORD himself will fight for you. You won't have to lift a finger in your defense!" (Exodus 14:13–14, NLT).

Even at the time, I believed the dream had been from the Lord. But I had just assumed God was giving me a heads-up that some adolescent challenges were on the way. He wanted to reassure me that He was going to be with us in the struggle, acting on our behalf.

I couldn't have guessed what God was really preparing me for.

I never imagined our story unfolding the way it did.

Going into high school, Jessie was an "A" student. It never crossed my mind that I'd ever be worried about her potential to graduate.

But God knew. He woke me up one sorrowful night to

remind me of an earlier dream and underlined His words of promise: *"She will be fine. It will be a fight, and I will do the fighting for you."* His words became a treasure in my darkness. A golden nugget I clung to throughout her senior year.

Graduation day came. On her way out the door to the coliseum, she called out, "Bring the video camera, Mom! I'm in a short drama that opens and closes the ceremony." Jessie paraded across the stage with the rest of her class as family and friends whooped and hollered from the grandstands.

I had a hard time seeing through the camera lens that day. Tears welled without warning as I watched the dream I'd had four years earlier come to pass right before my eyes. There she stood, onstage, addressing the audience. God had seen her through.

Sorrow hurts, but it doesn't harm. It slows us down to give us an opportunity to think seriously about our priorities. It does violence to selfish and superficial pursuits and reconfigures our outlook on reality. We discover that self-reliance and the well-intentioned efforts of others fall short while we walk the silent corridors of suffering.

Pain drives us into deep, dark places where only God can reach us. As we open our heart to Him, He assists us in separating from shattered dreams. As with the blind man along the road to Jericho, He graciously touches our eyes and enables us to see things we have never seen before. Taking us by the hand, He leads us to treasures that can only be witnessed with eyes of faith. Standing in our future, He calls us forward, bidding us to persist and endure.

Along the way we come to know His gentle touch. We sense His acquaintance with our grief. We experience Him as the God who binds up our wounds.

For now and forever.

1. When you think back over your life, which childhood loss was most painful? What helped you keep going? What did you learn from this dark time?

2. What was your family "rule" about coping with pain? (e.g., ignore it, stuff it, fake it, or express it) How does this rule affect you today?

3. Which of the "Myths about Grief" on page 60 do you tend to slip into?

4. Begin the process of letting go of your grief by writing down your most painful losses, then consider doing one of the following: burn your paper in the fireplace, shred your paper, or wrap your paper around a rock and throw it into a lake, river, or ocean.

Hidden Faces

[Steve]

These emotions—guilt and shame—
guide us to our better selves.

WILLARD GAYLIN

i hope nobody ever finds out."

"What are you afraid of?" I asked.

"They'd hate me," Allison said with sad resignation. "They'd reject me. They'd think I was the biggest loser of all time."

Her pain and fear permeated the room. I wanted to encourage and affirm her. I wanted to take away her hurt, but all I could think to say was, "But what if they forgave you?"

"But what if they *didn't*?" she shot back.

"What if you forgave yourself?"

"I don't know if I can." She grew quiet and reflective. Tears formed in her eyes but refused to fall. "It just feels too big. I wish I could go back and do everything over again."

I've had this conversation hundreds of times with hundreds of women about hundreds of wounds: from having an abortion to being raped; from dropping out of school to leaving a husband; from a best friend's suicide to a vicious eating disorder.

We all have sins and secrets and embarrassments that haunt us. These are wounds we intentionally hide behind nice clothing, bright smiles, hard work, good deeds—or anything else that will help us avoid disclosure.

Our wounds make us hypersensitive to guilt and shame. Most of us hide our pain. We don't want people to see our brokenness or failures. We all want to be loved and accepted. We all dream of being healthy.

One of the stories about Jesus that touches me the most is about an unnamed woman caught in guilt and shame.

It is early in the morning, before most people have headed off to work. Jesus has been teaching the last few days about living water, saying, "If you are thirsty, come to Me." A crowd has gathered to hear more, their throats dry as they yearn for hope.

Suddenly there is a disturbance—shouting and struggling. A panicked, half-dressed woman is being dragged down the cobblestone streets by strong men with stern faces. They push and shove her until she collapses in a heap before the curious crowd. She trembles as she covers her tear-stained face. Her hair is uncombed. Her feet are bleeding. Her dress is torn. She pulls it tighter around her shoulders to hide her nakedness. But she cannot hide her guilt and shame.

One of the men in authority shouts out the accusation:

"This woman was caught in the very act of adultery."

Caught: "We got you."

In the very act: "There's no getting out of this one!"

Adultery: "How dare you? What were you thinking?"

Men gathered stones—sizable, with sharp angles. Clutching them firmly in impatient fists, they waited for the signal. They knew what to do. Throwing stones came easy for them.

Jesus, however, didn't pick up His stone. Inexplicably, He bent down and began writing in the dust with His finger. Nobody knew what He wrote for sure, except those who encircled the wounded woman.

Some think He wrote something like "If you forgive others, you will be forgiven" (Luke 6:37, NLT). Others think He wrote in front of each man a personal example of his secret guilt or shame. *Laziness, pride, greed, abuse, dishonesty, addiction, hypocrisy.* But whatever He wrote, it had its impact. Finally looking up, He said, "Let those who have never sinned throw the first stones" (John 8:7, NLT).

Faces fell.

Hands loosened their grip.

Rocks dropped.

Sandaled feet left, one by one.

All was silent.

In a gentle voice Jesus asked, "Where are your accusers? Didn't even one of them condemn you?"

She looked into those dark eyes of compassion and mercy. "No, Lord."

"Neither do I. Go and sin no more."

She rose slowly to her feet, awash in a mixture of relief and amazement. Her guilt had been forgiven, her shame washed clean, her wounds healed. She had been set free. Now came her greatest challenge: She must live like it.

We are all like this woman in some way. Maybe our guilt and shame are still private. We know our failures, and we fear what might happen if they are discovered. Or maybe we've already been caught. We feel the panic and vulnerability of exposure. We see the crowd encircle us, clutching their sharp stones. A few of us have even felt the sting of those stones as friends and family and even strangers have let them fly.

Or maybe we've seen God's grace and heard "You are forgiven." Some of us have experienced the tender compassion and warm encouragement of others. We have experienced the freedom of another wounded woman who fell at Jesus' feet "and told him what she had done." Jesus reached out: "Go in peace. You have been healed" (Mark 5:33–34, NLT). This is the hope of all who have known the pain of being wounded.

We have to be on guard to keep our wounds from festering into guilt and shame. Closely related, these two intense emotions sometimes overlap. Yet they are distinctly different. Separate or combined, they form a powerful acid that can burn right through our peace and contentment. They can create great pain, disfiguring or destroying our plans and dreams.

But even acid has a purpose.

Sometimes it's needed to eat through harmful attitudes and hard, unyielding hearts.

Our wounds can trigger guilt. That guilt, if not dealt with, can become shame. Guilt tells us that we've thought, said, or done something wrong. As a result, we believe that we deserve some sort of punishment. Shame tells us that we're just plain bad people. Fearing rejection or punishment, we withdraw, hoping things won't get any worse. Yet that very withdrawal traps us in our guilt and shame.

Guilt

We are *all* guilty.

Let's get that out of the way right off the top.

The Bible tells us that "all have sinned; all fall short of God's glorious standard" (Romans 3:23, NLT).

Each one of us has thought, said, or done things that we have later regretted. A seven-year-old girl told her parents that she had to see Dr. Steve. They asked her why, and all she would say was "Something is wrong, but I can only tell Dr. Steve." Every day for two weeks she persistently said she had to see Dr. Steve.

Finally the parents brought her to my office, and the girl poured out her concerns: "*My brain is broken,*" she told me very seriously. "You know that thing in your head that keeps your thoughts from coming out your mouth? Well, it doesn't work for me. Whenever I think something bad, I just say it.

Then I feel so bad because I don't want to hurt people."

Maybe we all have broken brains.

When my son, Dusty, was nine, I asked him if he ever lied. Without hesitation he looked me in the eye and said, "Yes, because 'all have sinned and fallen short of the glory of God.'" Then he thought for a minute and said, "Dad, do you know why that's such a good verse?" I shook my head. "It's because you can use it whenever you're in trouble," he explained, adding, "and for me that's almost every day."

Guilt is a part of being human. It's a recognition of our brokenness and weakness. It's a reminder that we all are wounded.

Guilt is a good thing. Like a warning light on the instrument panel of your car, warning you that something is amiss. (And that warns us to consult our Manufacturer!) It tells us when we have done something hurtful to others, ourselves, or God. It's a signal that we have broken our value system and need to change our behavior. Guilt comes from a healthy conscience. We *should* feel guilty if we lie or cheat or steal.

Kylie was bright and articulate, but something about her left me deeply troubled: Kylie felt no guilt. None at all. She told me she loved her husband and that he was a good man, but she was sleeping with his best friend. This had been going on for about two years, and she had created an elaborate web of lies to protect herself from discovery. I was concerned about the affair, but I was more concerned with her lack of guilt and her twisted justifications.

"Sometimes things just happen."

"I couldn't help myself."

"He's better off not knowing."

"It's not like I'm hurting anybody."

"It's not my fault that he wouldn't understand."

"Some women just can't be faithful to only one man."

Kylie frightens me.

Think about it. Without guilt, she is capable of *anything*. There is nothing to stop her, no speed bumps to slow her down, no guardrails to keep her on the road. She can get out of control and not even know it…or care.

Extremes are rarely healthy. Too much guilt, like no guilt, can take you down a dangerous path. I know women who feel guilty for everything, from having been sexually abused to being "too emotional."

73

We live in a world of "shoulds," and if we do not meet our particular list of shoulds, we frequently feel guilty. Yet the real question is: "Are those shoulds of ours realistic or healthy or even possible?"

Should comes from the Anglo-Saxon word for *scold*. Too often we scold ourselves for not being perfect or not being able to make those around us happy. But nobody's perfect, so it's time to stop beating ourselves up.

A FEW COMMON "SHOULDS"

I should always be kind, patient, loving, and encouraging in every situation.

I should never make mistakes.

I should never forget.

*I should always be happy and positive and have a great
attitude.*

*I should be able to quickly find the best solution to
every problem.*

I should never be angry, frustrated, or lose my temper.

I should never hurt anybody.

I should always be prepared (for anything).

I should be a positive example in all I say and do.

I should never get sick or exhausted.

*I should be able to deal with any difficulty or trauma
with complete composure.*

I should never let people discourage or disappoint me.

I should never let my feelings control me.

I should always be perfect.

74

Healthy guilt keeps us in touch with reality. It reminds us of what is destructive to ourselves and those around us. Toxic guilt causes us to become fixated on our wounds—scratching them, picking off their scabs, poking and squeezing them—and not letting them heal. Toxic guilt makes a wound worse. Healthy guilt pushes us toward healing.

Corrie ten Boom once wrote: "The purpose of being guilty is to bring us to Jesus. Once we are there, then its purpose is over." Healthy guilt seeks forgiveness and freedom. It yearns for a fresh start, not through denial or minimization, but through repentance and repair.

King David wrote, "My guilt overwhelms me.… My wounds fester.… I am deeply sorry for what I have done" (Psalm 38:4, 5, 18, NLT). But he refused to let these things turn him into a bitter man. He cried out, "Come quickly to help me, O Lord my savior" (v. 22, NLT).

Turn your back on toxic guilt. And turn your healthy guilt over to God.

Shame

Unresolved guilt frequently ends up as shame.

When Brook was twenty-one, her husband left her two months after a large and elegant church wedding. He gave no reason—he just left and filed for divorce. Brook believed she must have done something wrong. After all, a bright and successful man wouldn't walk out if she was a good wife.

Several years later she moved to another community and married again. No one there knew her secret except her new husband. When an old friend came to visit and casually asked about her previous husband at a dinner party, Brook was mortified. Her face turned crimson with shame as she rushed from the room. Alone with her husband, she hid her face and said she could never face her friends again.

Shame keeps its head down. It believes that if others see our wounds they will have nothing to do with us. Shame tells us that our wounds make us totally worthless and unacceptable. Sandra Wilson writes that "shame is a strong sense of being uniquely and hopelessly different and less than other human beings." It says that if we are flawed, scarred, or limited, then there is nothing that can be done about us. It relegates us to the garbage heap with messages like "You are not good" or "You are not good enough." These messages get internalized, and shame begets shame.

SHAME'S TALK	GOD'S ANSWER
I am damaged.	I will heal you.
I am dirty.	I will wash you whiter than snow.
I am incompetent.	I will teach you all you need to know.
I am stupid.	I will fill you with wisdom.
I am unwanted.	I made you.
I am weak.	In your weakness I am made strong.
I am hopeless.	I will give you hope.
I am unlovable.	I sent My Son to die for you.
I am nothing.	You are My child.
I am worthless.	You are precious.

Shame often magnifies and exaggerates our wounds. It generalizes from our having specific wounds to proclaiming we are totally wounded. We now become a victim, and nothing more than a victim. Shame insists that our wounds now define every aspect of our identity. We can be nothing more than our wounds, and when people see us, that is all they will see. Yet this is paranoid thinking. If we strip shame of its exaggeration, we are left with five basic truths that shame is telling us. Shame is...

- ✹ a symptom that something is wrong

- ✹ a recognition of our limitations

- ✹ a reminder that we are flawed

- a defense against pride

- a chance to better understand our wounds

These perspectives allow our shame to be redemptive rather than destructive. God's grace is ultimately the best cure for debilitating shame, for it takes away the two things that give shame its power—rejection and abandonment. God's grace wraps us in unconditional love and acceptance.

So What Do We Do Now?

No matter how painful something is, we must face it. Ignoring a wound does not make it go away. Robert C. Larson wrote: "Unfriendly ghosts from your past may never disappear entirely. They can return to haunt you at a moment's notice. The key is to keep meeting these apparitions head-on...."

Stare straight into the dark eyes of your wounds— remembering the situations, experiencing the feelings, dealing with the guilt and shame. In *Healing of Memories*, David Seamonds writes, "The harder we try to keep bad memories out of conscious recall, the more powerful they become. Since they are not allowed to enter through the door of our minds directly, they come into our personalities (body, mind and spirit) in disguised and destructive ways."

By not facing our wounds boldly and directly, we may force them into the most negative forms of guilt and shame.

Yet as we face our wounds, we can turn them into teachers, and guilt and shame take the positive role of pulling us out of the shadows rather than pushing us into them.

Grace and forgiveness are the cures to our deepest guilt. The first step is to stop beating ourselves up for the past and to start forgiving ourselves. Maybe we need to forgive ourselves for what we did or what we didn't do. Sometimes we need to forgive ourselves for letting false guilt torture and paralyze us. If we are truly guilty, we must walk through the following:

- *Repentance:* Admit to ourselves and those impacted what we have thought, said, or done that was wrong.

- *Remorse:* Feel genuine, heartfelt sorrow for how we have hurt God, others, and ourselves.

- *Restitution:* Do something sacrificial that's related to our wrong and that shows we take what we have done seriously.

- *Repair:* Go to those we have wronged seeking forgiveness, and then make specific changes that will help protect us from repeating our wrong.

Now…release your guilt and as Jesus said to the woman caught in her shame, "Go and sin no more."

Forgiveness allows us to let go of the past and envision a new tomorrow. Forgiveness of others helps erase our shame. In every wound there are people to forgive:

- people who wounded us

- people who didn't protect us

- people who deepened our wounds

- people who didn't or wouldn't understand

- people who wouldn't help us heal

- people who judged us

Forgiving others detaches us from our guilt and shame. It lifts us above our wounds. Sure, some of these people don't deserve our forgiveness, but that's not the issue. Without forgiveness, we become trapped in vengeance or victimization. Forgiveness sets us free, and freedom allows us to use our pain to better ourselves and those around us.

As we forgive ourselves and others, we can freely embrace the forgiveness of God. David cries out, "O Lord, you are so good, so ready to forgive" (Psalm 86:5, NLT). All we need to do is ask with a sincere heart. God is willing to wash away our guilt and shame. The scars that remain are covered with His never-ending grace and touched with a divine meaning. As the playwright Eugene O'Neill once wrote, "Man is born broken. He lives by mending. Grace is the glue."

1. Which of the common "shoulds" on pages 73–74 have you told yourself in the last week?

2. How do these "shoulds" set you up for exhaustion and discouragement? What might you tell yourself that is more realistic?

3. How do bitterness and unforgiveness trap you in your hurt? Who might you need to forgive so that you can be freed from the past and set free for the future?

4. What did you notice about Jesus in the story of the woman who was caught in adultery? Have you experienced grace and forgiveness in your relationship with Him? If not, you might want to take a moment and talk to God about what's on your heart.

Facing Fears and Finding Peace

[Pam]

> The adventurous life is not one exempt from fear,
> but on the contrary, one that is lived in full
> knowledge of fears of all kinds, one in which
> we go forward in spite of our fears.
>
> PAUL TOURNIER

'm not picking up a heartbeat, Pam. There doesn't appear to be any fetal movement. I think the baby is dead."

In disbelief, my emotions began to run wild and unchecked. Engulfed in a jumble of scrambled thoughts, my heart raced, and I could barely catch my breath. The tears poured out. I sobbed long and hard that day, trying my best to cope with the shocking news. Our life journey had taken a sudden, sharp turn.

We had waited until I finished graduate school to start a family, and this baby was the answer to many prayers. I was on cloud nine wearing maternity clothes, decorating our nursery, and planning for our baby's arrival.

The pregnancy was progressing exceptionally well. I walked into my doctor's office for my fifth-month routine check, proudly wearing a new maternity dress.

The doctor walked into the room with a smile. "Let's listen to the heartbeat." It was like the first time all over again. I was so excited I embarrassed myself.

A few minutes passed. The Doppler ultrasound didn't seem to be picking up anything. I watched intently for some clue as to what was going on. The doctor's face was blank. The nurse was stoic. I began to feel scared, confusion replacing my happy excitement. Apprehension grew like a dark cloud rolling across the horizon, blocking the sunlight. They took me into another room, filled with foreign instruments and equipment. My arms and legs felt like they weighed two hundred pounds as I climbed up on the examining table.

There I sat...shaken and chilled.

The nurse probed with the sound device to secure a clear picture. And then the ripping truth came.

In the months that followed I was a different woman. My usual optimistic outlook on life was tainted by a foreboding sense of apprehension and anxiety. It's a fairly common experience among those who have been traumatized by stressful life events.

In the twenty-five years I've been a counselor, I think I've treated more people suffering with fear and anxiety than from any other problem. This parallels national statistics. Anxiety is the most common complaint heard by professional clinicians and the fifth most common complaint received by medical doctors.

One out of four Americans is diagnosed with an anxiety disorder during his or her lifetime. One-third of the general population experienced a panic attack in the last year. A panic attack occurs when the body goes into "fight or flight" mode, dumping hormones into the bloodstream that trigger heart palpitations, dry mouth, sweaty palms, racing thoughts, tightness in the chest, difficulty breathing, and an overwhelming sense of dread.

My interest in this disease of the soul is far more than professional. I have personally wrestled with anxiety on several levels. It can manifest itself as a simple case of the butterflies before I speak at a large conference. In this case the anxiety is positive—it triggers just enough adrenaline to allow keen concentration and peak performance. But when fear takes a stronger hold and leaves me with overramped nerves, a dry mouth, and "brain freeze," it's anything but positive. It's a real nuisance.

There have been times when anxiety has been more than just a pesky problem. It was more like a noose around my neck, progressively squeezing the life out of me. My first bout with heightened anxiety occurred after our first baby suddenly died in the womb halfway to term.

The next episode followed the traumatic birth of our youngest son, Nathan, who arrived six weeks early. When Nathan entered the world, I knew something was terribly wrong. He was blue, not breathing well, and his little cry sounded muted. Instead of laying him in my waiting arms, the technicians scurried around trying to suction his mouth to help him breathe. John held my hands and we prayed for Nathan, asking God to help him and to guide the doctors' efforts.

The pediatrician on call came over to talk with us. "Mrs. Vredevelt, your son is not oxygenating well, so we're trying to help him with oxygen and IVs."

"Is this life threatening?" I asked.

"It could be," she replied. "It's also my observation that he has Down syndrome. I've called a cardiologist to examine him because his heart isn't functioning properly. We have placed a catheter in his heart, and the technicians are still working to stabilize him."

The postpartum hormone changes combined with the astonishment of his medical conditions was like a bombshell exploding in my psyche. The trauma sent shock waves throughout my body and left me with a horrid case of anxiety that lasted well over a year.

My most recent angst began with the traffic accident we already described: the night when our daughter Jessie called to tell us she had been rear-ended by an eighteen-wheel semi truck on the freeway.

It hurts to see those you love hurt. The chronic strain of watching her suffer about did me in as a mom. There were times when I sincerely wondered if I could face another day. Without God, I probably would have caved in.

During these emotionally charged and distressing seasons, I used every resource I could find to help me understand and work with turbulent and unpredictable waves of emotion. Eventually, my body and my mind calmed down, but not nearly as quickly as I hoped, or as easily as I wanted. That's often the way it is with deep, long-lasting healing. The good news is, I can honestly say that healing did come, and—unless I'm unusually stressed—I don't feel emotionally fragile or on edge.

Wounds happen to all of us. Trauma strikes without warning. Because we live in a world filled with unpredictable and threatening situations often beyond our control, we will never eliminate our fears. But there are some time-tested and clinically proven strategies for facing our fears that can calm our nerves and lead us into peace.

Let's look at some of these together.

SEVEN WAYS TO INCREASE YOUR ANXIETY

1. Take things too seriously.

2. Avoid the situation that's bugging you.

3. Keep things trapped inside.

4. Imagine worst-case scenarios.

5. Try to handle everything on your own.

6. Wear yourself out.

7. Refuse to share your burdens with God.

Review the Facts

Naomi spoke with me one afternoon about the worries that tormented her. As we reviewed her history, I learned that a teenage neighbor boy had sexually violated her when she was seven years old. When she came to see me, her oldest son was in the first grade, and Naomi was extremely fearful that what had happened to her would also happen to him. Her concerns for her son were driven by her own childhood wound that had been hidden for years.

"Bobby keeps getting invitations to spend the night at his friends' homes," Naomi explained. "I can't let him go. I'm so afraid that something bad might happen to him." Naomi knew that her anxiety was blown out of proportion, but she still couldn't shake it. One of my goals was to help Naomi understand her fears.

"Naomi, the avoidance you're using to cope with these situations is actually driving your anxiety," I said. "This is not the kind of fear you can retreat from in the hope that it will just go away. If you want to beat this fear, you're going to have to face it head-on. You see, the fact is: *Avoidance increases anxiety.*"

Naomi spent the next few sessions in counseling revisiting and processing her childhood trauma. As she connected her current feelings with the facts of her abuse and grieved the injustice, the pain slowly but surely began to lose its power. To help separate the past from the present, Naomi made a list of the facts about her past experience. She then compared it with a list of the facts surrounding Bobby's life.

Seeing the specific differences in black and white brought her a measure of relief.

But there was more work to do. Naomi needed to review the facts with her son. She bought a children's book about personal safety and taught Bobby how to pay attention to the "uh-oh" in his tummy. He learned that it was very important to "Say no!" and to "Go and tell" an adult if he felt at risk. She rehearsed potential scenarios with Bobby and showed him how to respond to someone who was acting in a sexually inappropriate way. Giving Bobby the facts reduced Naomi's concerns about his vulnerability and increased her confidence in his ability to protect himself.

Gathering facts about Bobby's friends and their parents was also helpful. Naomi felt more comfortable with some individuals than with others. She reached a great milestone when she and her husband gave Bobby permission to spend the night with his best friend after a ball game. It didn't happen without some anxiety, but it happened!

Is fear stealing your joy? Are anxieties eating away at your peace of mind? If so, may I make a suggestion? Please—get the facts. If you're fretting about the possibility of a health problem, don't brood over it. Call a doctor or see a specialist who can review the facts with you.

Focus your attention on what is, not on what if.

Face your fears. Investigate. Ask questions. Research. Pool information. A mind that feeds on the facts is less likely to fall prey to a frenzied imagination that casts illusions as reality. The fear of the unknown can paralyze you, but reviewing the facts puts you in a good position to take the next step.

Billy Graham once said, "Peace is not arbitrary. It must be based upon definite facts. God has all the facts on His side; the world does not. Therefore God, and not the world, can give peace."

Reconnect with the Present

Years ago I saw a clever acrostic for the word *fear*:

False **E**vidence **A**ppearing **R**eal.

When fearful, we rarely think clearly. It's easy to jump to conclusions. Anxiety can short-circuit the brain, leading us to misinterpret the meaning of an event and to envision all manner of exaggerated worst-case scenarios.

I've heard it said that the more intelligent and creative you are, the more likely you are to worry. Why? Because when we worry about something, our imagination paints pictures in our mind of what we dread most. People with sharp minds see all the angles of a given predicament, and their creative component enables them to vividly envision every possible miserable outcome. (Moral of the story: Be glad if you weren't born intelligent and creative!)

Many of our worries come from a tendency to overestimate the probability of a harmful event and to exaggerate its potential negative impact. Seeking to peer into the future, our imagination runs wild, leading us to conclude that things are going to turn out badly and with unbearable results.

One of the best ways to stop this needless waste of mental and emotional energy is to live in the moment.

Not tomorrow.

Not next week.

Not next month.

But today, right now.

I know—it's easier said than done. The human mind likes to wander from the present, particularly when our thought processes aren't focused on something stimulating.

During the year following Jessie's accident, this mental discipline became my daily assignment. Very intentionally, I had to work at reeling in my imagination to keep it in the here and now. Some days I did this better than others. When I wasn't proactive with this, worry took its toll. One afternoon my massage therapist was working on my shoulders.

"Pam," she said, "these muscles feel like you've been trying to carry the weight of the world. Are you burdened about something?"

My body never lies. It sends clear cues about what is going on in my mind.

"Yes, Trish," I confessed. "It's the 'mom thing.' I'm worried about Jessie…." I didn't have to say another word. She knew about the accident. And being the mom of a daughter who is blind, she also understood the stress of living with difficult situations that aren't easily resolved. She continued the therapy, moving on to my legs.

"Ouch, that hurts!" I blurted out as she worked her thumbs into my calf muscles. My legs are usually not a problem area because I power walk four days a week and stretch my calves afterward. Lightening her touch, she gently said, "Pam, you're probably just walking into the future too much...."

I've never forgotten that comment. It was a powerful reminder to me of the mind-body connection and my need to live in the present. In the silence of that moment I prayed, *God, I'm leaving the future alone and tucking in close to You. With You, I can handle today. With You, I can face tomorrow. With You, my children will fulfill the plans and purposes for their lives. I choose to rest in You..."*

Our thoughts influence our feelings. In a matter of seconds, they can destroy our peaceful state of mind and create panicked anxiety without anything else changing around us. The opposite is also true. Bringing our thoughts out of the future and into the present can calm and quiet our nerves. Some of our most important thoughts are those that contradict our emotions.

I've found that we fearful people often deny ourselves entry through the doors that lead us to healing and growth. We cower lest we make one more mistake or open ourselves up to something that will cause our demise. So we hunker down in our pain and terror and attempt to survive our self-imposed isolation. We cry out that we want to be different, yet we refuse to budge from our atrophied existence.

—PATSY CLAIRMONT

Refuse to Assume the Worst

After any situation in which our mind is overtaxed for a prolonged period of time, our psychological defenses are weak and we find it difficult to ward off worries. Anxious thoughts that would typically bounce off of us during less stressful times seem to penetrate and stick. Once they stick, they grow, and we lose an accurate perspective of what's really happening around us.

One of the best ways to manage worries that are multiplying exponentially is simply to interrupt the process in your head by saying firmly, "Stop it!" Assertively halt the escalating thoughts, and remember the Lord's desire to bring perspective and peace to your heart. The psalmist wrote: "When my anxious thoughts multiply within me, Your consolations delight my soul" (Psalm 94:19, NASB).

I remember well the year after Nathan was born. Grieving his Down syndrome and worrying about the holes in his heart, I found myself sliding into a dark funk. The facts set me up to worry. We had lived through the death of one baby, and Nathan's heart condition was serious. Under the circumstances, I suppose it wasn't all that odd that I battled with intrusive fears of finding him dead in his crib.

When we are worried our imagination runs wild. And the more it does, the more anxious we feel. It's a vicious spiral. But the spiral can be interrupted. We can say "stop" to our thoughts. We can test reality and refuse to let little things become big things.

Time and again when the thought of losing Nathan entered my mind, I said, "Stop! That's a wild imagination. I'm *not* going down that road. Nathan is sleeping peacefully. His color is good. He's breathing well. He's fine. I refuse to make this a big deal. And besides, God controls the number of days Nathan has in this world."

And do you know what? The gloomy thoughts stopped and my anxiety gradually faded. The good news is we don't have to compulsively follow every train of thought that enters our head. Jump off the train and let it go! A thought is simply a thought. We don't have to give it more power than it deserves.

The question is, where are we going to fix our thoughts? The apostle Paul encourages us: "Fix your thoughts on what is true and honorable and right. Think about things that are pure and lovely and admirable. Think about things that are excellent and worthy of praise.… And the *God of peace* will be with you" (Philippians 4:8–9, NLT, emphasis mine).

Paul even suggests formatting our thoughts so that we can live in the present, experiencing God's peace. He writes, "Don't worry about anything; instead, pray about everything. Tell God what you need, and thank him for all he has done. If you do this, you will experience God's peace, which is far more wonderful than the human mind can understand. *His peace* will guard your hearts and minds" (vv. 6–7, emphasis mine). It comforts me to know that I don't have to create my own peace. God will do this for me. The sage old prophet Isaiah boldly proclaimed: "You will keep in perfect peace all who trust in you, whose thoughts are fixed on you!" (Isaiah 26:3, NLT).

Speaking on a relational level, the Bible says, "Pursue peace with all men" (Hebrews 12:14, NASB). But when it comes to peace in our heart, peace at the core of our being, peace isn't something we can chase down like some rare butterfly. In fact, it is a *by-product*. It is a stabilizing energy, as real as the energy of electricity, that God's Spirit imparts to our spirit when we deliberately adjust our thoughts to His wise counsel. It comes when we face our fears and review the facts. When we reconnect with the present. When we refuse to assume the worst. When we fix our thoughts on God and trust Him with everything that concerns us.

He loves you, and longs to be your peace.

> The LORD gives his people strength.
>
> The LORD blesses them with peace.
> (Psalm 29:11, NLT)

1. On a scale of one to ten (with ten being most intense), where is your anxiety level right now? Which of the seven ways to increase your anxiety listed on page 85 do you tend to use the most?

2. What do you commonly worry about the most? One way to reduce your anxiety is to review the facts. Make a list of all the facts related to your worry.

3. Cindy Morgan said, "Fear is a thief. It robs you of a happy future. It also robs you of the moment that is before you. I wasted too many years being anxious, panicked, and fearful, and lost too many potentially wonderful moments." Identify a time in your life when fear robbed you of a potentially wonderful experience.

4. Go to a local café with a good friend and ask him or her to help you sort through the realistic and irrational aspects of your worst fear. Then go home and treat yourself to a nap, a warm bath, or a good book with a latte.

Letting Go of Anger

[Pam]

It is better to be patient than powerful;
it is better to have self-control than to conquer a city.

KING SOLOMAN

i was furious!"

Doug's confession about his affairs blew Kathy's world apart. Something in her died. Anger and resentment smothered her beneath their load. She seriously wondered if she would ever be able to dig her way out from under these harsh realities.

Shortly thereafter Doug moved out. He said he didn't love her and that he never really had. With few marketable skills, Kathy was forced to look for a job. For the last eight years she had devoted herself to staying home with the children.

By far, the most agonizing part of the whole tragedy was watching her children suffer. They were broken by the sorrow of this fragmented marriage and the uncertainty of the ongoing separation. Crumpling into a heap on the bathroom floor, Kathy begged God for strength to cope with the bone-crushing weariness of holding her little family together.

Each time Kathy confronted Doug about his sexual addiction, he simply shrugged it off. Convinced he didn't have a problem, he had no intention of changing. It became clear to Kathy that God's hands were tied. He could not heal where dishonesty reigned. Lies blocked His miracles. God lifted the blinders from Kathy's eyes and showed her she was absolutely powerless over Doug's choices. She filed for divorce and chose to remain silent about his infidelities.

Kathy had long, angry talks with God and asked hard, honest questions: *Where were You when Doug was betraying me? Why didn't You protect the children and me from this abuse? How could You allow this to happen? Will I ever be able to trust anyone again?*

All the while, God listened patiently and continued sending blessings that were difficult for Kathy to see through her pain. Overcome with the injustice she and her children had suffered, Kathy began to think about vengeance. By simply opening her mouth and telling her story, she knew she could destroy Doug.

Anger. Resentment. Rage. These are normal reactions when we are wounded. Betrayal and loss violate our sense of justice. In fury we cry, "This isn't fair!" Hanging on to anger and seeking vengeance can seem like a practical solution. It isn't. But neither is denying or stuffing our anger.

Unfortunately, many of us have been conditioned to

believe that anger—*all* anger—is bad. The truth is, it's okay to get angry. Anger is a part of our God-given emotional makeup. "Go ahead and be angry. You do well to be angry—but don't use your anger as fuel for revenge" (Ephesians 4:26, *The Message*).

If we deny or stuff our anger, we will end up feeling tired and bitter. Feelings that are pushed down and buried don't really die…they just go underground into hiding. I've met people who have hidden their feelings for so long that when they try to access them, they can't. They may not feel much anger, but they have no joy, either. Over time they become walking time bombs on the verge of exploding.

Anger is part of God's original design. Time and again in the Bible we find that Jesus was moved with "compassion" when He crossed paths with the wounded. The word *compassion* literally means to experience a gut-wrenching sensation. His heart broke when He saw people in desperate need, unfairly oppressed, or grossly mistreated. A strong sense of empathy led Him to feed the hungry, heal the sick, comfort the mourning, and raise the dead. He was angered and grieved over the injustices He witnessed. And His anger drove Him to take action on behalf of others.

Yes, Jesus got angry, but He used His anger as God intended—for good.

Those who are angry about the wounds they and others have suffered often make our world a better place to live. Martin Luther's anger about the religious abuses of his time ushered in the Reformation. The Thirteenth

Amendment was the fruit of agitation by abolitionists who were angry about the enslavement of human beings. Suffragists angry about being denied the vote initiated a campaign that resulted in the passage of the Nineteenth Amendment. Martin Luther King Jr.'s anger about racism led to the Civil Rights Act of 1964. All these people were angry, but they channeled their anger into positive action that brought about social reform.

When wounded, we must give ourselves permission to acknowledge and externalize our anger in positive ways. Anger is energy that can drive us forward in the grief process and help us come to terms with the injustices we've suffered. It's a powerful force that can ignite significant and long-lasting change.

Anger properly channeled and controlled is a good thing—a God-given thing. Like a gas flame on the stove, anger is not inherently destructive. It's a legitimate emotion that has a legitimate function. But it can be helpful or harmful, depending on how we use it. If we don't learn how to process and express it in healthy ways, the results can be ruinous. Aristotle said it well: "Anybody can become angry—that is easy; but to be angry with the right person, and to the right degree, and at the right time, and for the right purpose, and in the right way—that is not easy."

One tried-and-true strategy for working with anger is what we call the Triple P Method. It's a helpful way to remain calm when you feel as though your anger is escalating to a potentially dangerous level. The Triple P Method stands for three action steps: Pause. Ponder. Pray.

Pause

The first step is to deliberately stop, breathe deeply, and allow that boiling energy to drain away. Buy yourself some time. This lets your body and emotions cool down before you take action. You may even want to take a break and get away from whatever situation might be triggering your anger.

Have you ever noticed that the angrier we feel, the dumber we get? It's not only a perception; it's a proven fact. Anger reduces the oxygen to the brain, and our thinking gets foggy. When we're angry, we do ourselves a favor to pause, disengage from whatever might be fueling our fire, and calm ourselves down.

With emotional pressure building and swirling at high speed, the internal energy will be seeking a release. If we don't purposely open a release valve and let some of it out, we can become like a pressure cooker on the verge of exploding. But if we pause, we give ourselves a chance to let go of some of this pent-up energy.

The following list has some good ideas for discharging inner tension…before it explodes! Here are seven ways to trigger a calm response.

1. Take in a deep breath, count to five, then slowly let it out, and relax. (Old advice, but it still works!)

2. Tune in to your body and deliberately relax whatever is tense.

3. Walk around the room and shake out the tension.

4. Get a drink of water.

5. Lean back in your chair in a relaxed fashion.

6. Massage the back of your neck and shoulders.

7. Warm a heating pad and place it on your shoulders or lower back.

Ponder

Anger doesn't have to escalate. We can choose cool words over hot words when we talk to ourselves about what might be bothering us or driving our feelings of frustration. Self-awareness is an important key to managing anger because it allows us to monitor our tension and effectively release it. People who are skilled in managing their anger do this almost intuitively. They have a keen awareness of what is bothering them, and purposely turn down the heat on their anger so that it doesn't burn them or boil over onto others.

This has tremendous power to reduce tension and help us cope in the heat of the moment. Even hot anger doesn't have to boil over. Cool words can keep our anger in check and prevent us from fueling fires that harm ourselves or others.

COOL WORDS TO USE WHEN YOU'RE ANGRY

> *Getting angry won't get me what I want in the long run.*
>
> *Think straight. Keep focused. Stay positive.*
>
> *Keep reason and respect number one.*
>
> *Don't blame. Look for solutions.*
>
> *This situation isn't worth a coronary.*
>
> *This problem is annoying, but it doesn't have to be a big deal.*
>
> *I don't have to take this personally.*
>
> *What seems so important today won't seem so a few months from now.*
>
> *I can pick my fights and save my energy for more important issues.*
>
> *When the time is right, talk slow...talk soft.*

Pray

When we talk to God about our wounds and our anger, we do so for our sake, not His. He already knows the secrets of our heart. I'm not talking about prayers consisting of fancy, pious, religious words. I'm talking about authentically sharing our thoughts and feelings with God, as we would with our safest and most trusted friend. Some of the best prayers have more feelings than words. Whispers in the dark, cries from a lonely heart, sighs of confusion, and fumbling utterances offered to God will find their way to His ears, and He will answer.

Meanwhile, the moment we get tired in the waiting, God's Spirit is right alongside helping us along.
If we don't know how or what to pray, it doesn't
matter. He does our praying in and for us, making
prayer out of our wordless sighs, our aching groans.
He knows us far better than we know ourselves.
(Romans 8:26–27, *The Message*)

David, author of many of the psalms, mastered the art of
venting his anger in prayer. I love his bold honesty with God:

My enemies shout at me, making loud and wicked
threats. They bring trouble on me, hunting me
down in their anger.... Destroy them, Lord, and
confuse their speech, for I see violence and strife....
Let death seize my enemies by surprise; let the grave
swallow them alive, for evil makes its home within
them.... I will call on God, and the LORD will rescue me. Morning, noon, and night I plead aloud in
my distress, and the LORD hears my voice. He rescues me and keeps me safe from the battle waged
against me, even though many still oppose me....
Give your burdens to the LORD, and he will take
care of you. (Psalm 55:3, 9, 15–18, 22, NLT)

Rather than taking matters into his own hands, David
dumped his anger into God's lap, or as it says in *The
Message*, he piled his troubles on God's shoulders (Psalm

55:22). He asked God to take up his cause and bring revenge. His example challenges us. When we are angry, we feel a natural compulsion to act fast. We are driven to "set things straight" and balance the scales. It's basic human nature to want to reestablish justice in an unfair situation. Rather than depending on God, we take over. Our sense of justice screams, "If anything is going to be made right, I have to make it happen!"

The ways of the world are very different from the ways of God. We are advised to leave the how and when of revenge to God: "Do not repay anyone evil for evil.… Do not take revenge, my friends, but leave room for God's wrath, for it is written: 'It is mine to avenge; I will repay,' says the Lord.… Do not be overcome by evil, but overcome evil with good" (Romans 12:17, 19, 21). Someone once said, "He who seeks revenge digs two graves."

103

Justice will reign. God will initiate it, and God will complete it. He will either do it now, or He will do it later. It is God's promise to us. God is our avenger, right now, this very moment. Jesus stands today in the Father's presence as our Advocate. "We have one who speaks to the Father in our defense—Jesus Christ, the Righteous One" (1 John 2:1). The Holy Spirit is alongside us like legal counsel in a court case, representing us and fighting for our best interests: "The Spirit himself intercedes for us" (Romans 8:26).

I have talked often with God about these truths during difficult times in my life. Prayers based on these ideas have tempered my anger over setbacks and losses, reminding me of the bigger picture. Ultimately there is no situation in life that can defeat us because of who God is *in* us. He is greater than what assails us. He is more powerful than those who wound us. His plans and purposes for our life cannot be thwarted by anyone or anything, no matter how black things may seem.

Every pain, every sorrow, every ounce of anger surrendered to God will not be wasted. He takes it all—the good, the bad, the outrageously unfair—and puts a positive spin on it so that it ultimately works for our eternal good. "And we know that God causes everything to work together for the good of those who love God and are called according to his purpose for them" (Romans 8:28, NLT).

Henri Nouwen, one of my favorite authors, was a Catholic priest who taught at Yale and Harvard and traveled the world as a renowned author and lecturer. At the height of his career, he left behind prestige and power to serve severely handicapped people in France and Canada.

I have recorded many of Mr. Nouwen's reflections in my journal because of the hope his eternal perspectives offer. Reflecting on Christ's teaching about the suffering we encounter in this world, he describes our heartache as akin to birth pains: "And so, what seems a hindrance becomes a way; what seems an obstacle becomes a door; and what seems a misfit becomes a cornerstone. Jesus changes our history from a random series of sad incidents and accidents into a constant opportunity for a change of heart."

In this sense, any pain we surrender to God serves an

eternal purpose. Freedom comes as we refuse to rehearse the wrongs committed against us and we let go of our insatiable hunger to get even.

Renounce Replays and Revenge

Replays don't divert anger; they sustain and fuel it. Our mind plays reruns of those wretched events connected with our wounds over and over and over again. Many of the replays are laced with fantasies of retribution. With each painful image, our dreams of retaliation grow crueler, and the chance that we will act on our anger increases.

Every angry scene we relive pushes the adrenaline button in our body and throws us into "fight or flight" mode all over again. The more we rehearse our pain and fantasize revenge, the more we weaken our ability to control our impulses and set ourselves up to act in ways that can destroy us. Thoughts of being burned, cheated, and demeaned drive feelings of anger, humiliation, and hate…and trap us in a torture chamber of our own making.

But we don't have to live at the mercy of the violent images that keep us chained to our pain. We don't have to be victimized by runaway fantasies that poison our soul with bitterness and hatred. There's a way to put an end to the hostile nightmares. There's an alternative to clinging to our lust for revenge.

It's called forgiveness.

Forgiveness is surrendering my right to hurt you for hurting me. It is the hallmark of the Christian faith. As Chuck Colson says, "Nothing is more Christian than forgiveness."

One thing is certain: We cannot overcome evil with evil; we can only overcome evil with good (see Romans 12:21). God is good, and He instructs us to forgive—not for His sake, not for the sake of the one who wounded us, but for ours. It is God's required course because He knows that forgiveness is in our best interest and a critical key to our full recovery.

Forgiveness and letting go of anger are one and the same. If we do not forgive, we sentence ourselves to a life imprisoned by pain. We freeze ourselves in the past, weigh ourselves down with heavy grudges, and become arrested in our grief. And we give our betrayers more power than they deserve by allowing them to repeatedly frustrate and immobilize us.

Frankly, even the thought of forgiving a person who has wounded us can make us angry. We don't *want* to forgive because we don't want to let them off the hook.

Forgiveness is neither easy nor natural.

It is difficult and supernatural.

Forgiveness requires God's involvement. The more we've been hurt, the more we need God's grace to forgive.

How do you forgive when your emotions are screaming revenge? A simple, glib "I forgive you" rarely cuts it. Forgiveness is an intentional choice of the will that encompasses a process. As we move through the process step-by-step, we gradually sense God's creative work in our heart, relieving our pain and restoring our joy. Here are several steps to help you experience the freedom of forgiveness.[1]

Step One: Admit the hurt and anger.

There is a place where the process of healing and forgiveness must begin. That place is honesty. You don't want to minimize what happened, but you don't want to exaggerate it either. Truthfully look at what, if any, part you contributed to the problem. Writing down your memories and feelings about an event can give you added insight. This first step proves to be the most difficult for many…and the most freeing. Don't be surprised if it opens a floodgate of unshed tears. And that's okay. Because feeling is healing, remember?

Step Two: Talk it out.

If you are in an ongoing relationship with someone who has hurt you, it's important that you talk about that hurt. Try to choose a convenient time and a private place. You will want to be open and honest and calmly express your perspective on what happened. Invite the other person to do the same. Remember, there are two sides to every story. Seeing the other side may not reduce the pain, but it may help you forgive.

If a face-to-face meeting is not possible or advisable, then find a safe person with whom you can dialogue about the wound. Be specific about the hurt you have suffered and how it has affected you. Peace and healing come in the context of safe relationships when we speak the truth in love (see Ephesians 4:15).

Step Three: Remind yourself that forgiveness is necessary for your freedom.

"Be kind to each other, tenderhearted, forgiving one another, just as God through Christ has forgiven you" (Ephesians 4:32, NLT).

The last part of this verse tells us why we need to forgive others. The truth is, we all carry the weight of the careless, hurtful, or terribly wrong things we have done, and we all have abundant need of forgiveness. The amazing thing is that when we come to God, confess our sin, and ask forgiveness...He forgives us. The Bible says it clearly: "If we confess our sins to him, he is faithful and just to forgive us and to cleanse us from every wrong" (1 John 1:9, NLT).

Jesus died to pay the price of our mistakes, and He longs for us to accept His free gift of forgiveness.

But He wants something else, too.

He wants us to forgive others—and not because they deserve it. Many of the offenders who have inflicted us with deep wounds don't deserve forgiveness. We know this...and God knows this even better. Nevertheless, He asks us to forgive because He forgave us first. Accepting God's forgiveness and forgiving others are both necessary if we want to experience full and complete healing.

Step Four: Ask God to empower you to make the choice to forgive.

Did you catch that? Forgiveness is a *choice*, a decision of the will. It really has very little to do with our feelings—feelings that can peak or plunge within a five-minute time interval. When we make the choice to forgive, we may still feel angry or resentful. Some wounds are so deep that it's virtually impossible to get beyond these intense emotions on our own. When this is the case, we need to ask God to supernaturally empower us. A practical place to start is with a simple prayer: "God, help me to be willing to forgive. Enable me to do what is right, even though my emotions are pushing me in the opposite direction." I have never met a person who has prayed that prayer and not found freedom. God will always empower us to do what He asks of us.

When we make the intentional choice to forgive, we open the door for God to do a creative miracle in our heart. Forgiveness gives Him access to our wound, and He heals, restores, and redeems what has been stolen from us. This is true even if nothing changes circumstantially or with those who have wounded us.

Step Five: Put the past behind you.

There is no such thing as "forgiving and forgetting."

Whoever came up with that pat little phrase was either dreaming, disingenuous, or a resident of the back side of the moon. Let's face it, once memories are logged in our mental computer, they're there for life. Thankfully, "forgetting" is not a prerequisite for healing our wounds—nor is it necessary for forgiveness. What *is* necessary is that we face the facts of our wounds, feel the feelings connected with those facts, express those feelings in constructive ways with God and safe people, and choose to relinquish replays and revenge.

Memories will rise in our mind (count on it), but we can choose to say, "I've handed that over to God. He's in charge of it now." Then we intentionally focus on other things.

Step Six: Be patient with the process.

Give yourself grace. It takes time for painful memories to lose their power, even when we have chosen to forgive. In time, however, our heart catches up with our head, and we sense new measures of freedom.

The process of forgiveness is sometimes complicated by recurring offenses. This is almost inevitable in close relationships such as marriage. In the cycle of hurt, forgiveness, and renewed trust, forgiveness must be repeated over and over again. It is a discipline we exercise daily. When relationships are restored through the process of giving and receiving forgiveness, they become more durable and intimate.

Sometimes, however, the direction to go when a person isn't sorry, won't stop offending, or is dedicated to our demise is detachment. In cases of repeated mistreatment or abuse, even though we choose to forgive, choosing to trust may be inappropriate or unsafe. It isn't wise to trust those who are not trustworthy. Trust must be earned. In these situations it is imperative to temporarily disengage from those who are inflicting wounds and to seek help from a pastor or trained professional. A bit of distance can help you sort through what you need in order to move forward in your personal healing and future reconciling with the person who wounded you.

When others hurt us in ways we don't deserve, at some point we will come to the crossroads of decision. We will have to look our pain square in the face and ask, *Am I going to hang on to my anger and do violence to myself, or am I going to forgive those who have wounded me? Am I going to allow bitterness to poison and putrefy my soul, or am I going to invite God to empower me to let the anger go?*

For every wounded woman, the glorious gifts of forgiveness are newfound freedom and relief. As we practice the work of letting go of our anger, we discover more and more that forgiveness and healing are one.

1. Circle four of the following expressions of anger you identify with the most.

resentment	hurt
irritation	disappointment
frustration	fury
rage	bugged
agitation	ticked-off

2. Anger is a secondary emotion. What rejection, attack, or threat might be driving your anger?

3. How has holding on to anger stunted your growth or blocked your forward movement? How has your anger affected those closest to you?

4. Using the three P's—Pause, Ponder, Pray— identify one source of anger and apply the process.

The Art of Overcoming

[Steve]

Although the world is full of suffering,
it is also full of the overcoming of it.

HELEN KELLER

L ife was a nightmare.

Stormie was physically and emotionally abused as a child. Her family was desperately poor, her mother was mentally ill, her peers ridiculed her. Stormie tried to escape through alcohol, drugs, and the occult. She lived a life of fear, loneliness, and self-hatred. This led to an abortion, a divorce, and major health problems. Life seemed to spiral out of control.

Stormie writes, "With me there was irreparable damage…I found it increasingly difficult to cope with life. The emptiness and pain I felt deepened each year. My periods of depression got worse, the anxiety within me increased, and suicidal thoughts met me every morning when I awoke."

At twenty-eight, Stormie Omartian decided she was tired of being a victim and was going to do something about it. She knew that if she continued to focus on her wounds, they would destroy her. She was scared, burned out, and miserable.

So she turned to God and she turned to the positive. After that moment, everything began to change. It didn't happen overnight, but healing came, one layer at a time.

Today, Stormie is one of the most positive people I've met. Her wounds are behind her, and she has decided to be an encourager of others. She is a songwriter, recording artist, and a successful author of books such as *The Power of a Praying Wife*. Refusing to let her past destroy her, Stormie wrote: "I have a burning desire to tell people who are hurting that there is a way out of their pain…hope for their lives."[2]

Stormie knows because she has been there.

Wounds breed negativity, and negativity can become more damaging than the wounds themselves. As Dale Galloway says: "In the final analysis, it is your own attitude that will make or break you, not what has happened to you."

Your attitude has incredible power. A positive attitude strengthens your faith, deepens your peace, adds to your joy, and improves your general health.

When we're struggling with severe pain, however, we don't even want to talk about a "positive attitude." The whole topic seems forced and shallow—and miles and miles distant from our real, hurting world.

Maybe so.

But remaining negative is a dangerous business.

Negativity is a whirlpool that can easily pull you into its vortex and drown you in its darkness. Over the years I have discovered the following four basic facts about negativity:

⚘ *Negativity comes naturally.* We don't have to work at it! It's more like a reflex reaction when we're hurting. The more extensive our wounds, the stronger and more long lasting our negative mindset. Becoming positive takes an intentional and determined effort. In fact, it takes the power of God Himself.

⚘ *Negativity makes us feel worse.* Negative feelings may come easily, but they're poison to us. They intensify our pain and can trap us in the dark hole of depression.

⚘ *Negativity pushes people away.* Most people steer clear of those who are consistently downbeat, negative, or cynical. This leaves us isolated and lonely. It causes us to feel even more worthless. Sadly, it also distances us from those we need the most.

⚘ *Negativity keeps us from healing.* Negativity keeps us focused on our wounds. It exaggerates the pain. When we are positive, we search for help and focus on hope.

Where we focus determines how we think and how we feel. Over time our thoughts and feelings will shape who we are and what our future looks like.

To be positive we must be intentional. We can't control our past wounds or our current circumstances or the people around us. But we can control our attitude. Attitude is everything. Some people consider it the single most important factor in their life. Patricia Neal writes that "a strong positive mental attitude will create more miracles than any wonder drugs."

Some people are born more optimistic. They find a silver lining in every cloud and see the glass half full. As in the Ronald Reagan joke of old, they'll dig through a roomful of manure believing "there must be a pony in here someplace." They bounce back from difficulties and have a sunny disposition on the gloomiest of days.

Then there are those who feel like a dark cloud always hangs over them. It's hard for them to look at the bright side of things. Whether being positive comes naturally or not, anyone can learn or develop the skill of optimism.

Let Go of the Hurt

The healthy person refuses to let past hurts destroy the good that happens today. An ancient Japanese proverb says: "Let the past drift away with the water." Leave the past to the past. What has happened may have been tragic, but to let it mar the future is even more tragic. The prophet Isaiah says to "forget the former things; do not dwell on the past" (Isaiah 43:18).

Kayla was abandoned by her mother. By the time she was fourteen, she had been in eight different foster homes and twelve different schools. When she was fifteen she ran away and lived on the streets for a year. Angry, depressed, and hopeless, one day she realized she had become a victim—and that made her even more angry.

"I've seen too many victims," she told me, "and they are pathetic. I refuse to be a victim." Now at age twenty-two, Kayla is active in a college-age group in her church and enrolled in a nursing program at her local community college. When I asked the secret of her overcoming the anger and depression, she said: "Realize that you can't change what happened, but you don't have to be a victim of it."

The more we focus on the wounds of the past, the more we are victimized by them. Victims fall into the following traps.

- They are overwhelmed by the negative.
- They get stuck in the negative.
- They think of themselves as negative.
- They see the future as negative.
- They believe there's no way out of the negative.

To escape a victim's attitude, we must squelch all the negative self-talk about the past.

Tell Yourself the Truth

We are constantly talking to ourselves. This self-talk shapes our perceptions and emotions. To become positive, we must stop our negative self-talk. The apostle Paul wrote

"Let everything you say be good and helpful" (Ephesians 4:29, NLT). This can just as easily relate to what we say to ourselves as to what we say to others.

Words have power. Our words matter. *Even the words we speak to and about ourselves in the silence of our thoughts.* Such words will either build us up or tear us down.

Negative self-talk looks at our wounds and says things like:
God is punishing me.
I deserve this.
Life is unfair.
I hate myself.
Nothing ever changes.
I am trapped.
There is no hope.

Negative statements make us feel more miserable. They reinforce the "victim mentality" and suck us deeper into the quicksand of dark thoughts and defeatist attitudes. They cause us to feel sorry for ourselves and develop a distorted image of reality. They become a self-fulfilling prophecy that makes everything worse.

Positive self-talk is like a safety line that can pull us out of despair. William James wrote that we "can alter [our] lives by altering [our] attitudes of mind." We change our attitudes by making positive and true statements to ourselves. In this way we follow the counsel of the apostle Paul, who wrote, "Let God transform you into a new person by changing the way you think" (Romans 12:2, NLT).

Repeating phrases like the following changes the way we think:

> *God loves me.*
> *With God all things are possible.*
> *God wants the best for me.*
> *God will strengthen me.*
> *This world is temporary.*
> *I am never trapped.*
> *I can be content, regardless of my circumstances.*

Positive self-talk can change our attitude, and with a changed attitude, everything looks different.

119

Hold on to the Lesson

Our wounds teach us powerful lessons. As Benjamin Franklin said: "The things which hurt, instruct." Hurts and difficulties are possibly the very best experiences we can have. And though we often resent them and see them as negatives, they are truly treasures. Harriet Beecher Stowe, author of *Uncle Tom's Cabin*, writes: "I long to put the experience of fifty years at once into your young lives, to give you at once the key to that treasure chamber every gem of which has cost me tears and struggles and prayers, but you must work for these inward treasures yourself."

Wounds have lessons to teach, and it's sad when we endure all of that pain but miss the valuable truth we might have drawn from our suffering. They aren't easy lessons—not by any means—yet even so, they are precious. Like the twists and turns which give the grain in wood character, so our wounds give us a depth and richness like nothing else does.

Karen Blixen had three loves in her life. Yet each left deep wounds. Her father committed suicide when she was ten. Her husband was continually unfaithful and gave her syphilis, which had no effective treatment at that time. After eleven years in an unhappy marriage, they divorced. Then she fell in love with a man who was gay. For thirteen years he was her best friend, yet unable to return her love. When she was forty-six, he was killed in an airplane crash.

In spite of these tragedies, Karen kept a positive attitude. She wrote many books under her pen name, Isak Dinesen, such as *Out of Africa* and *Winter's Tales*. In reflecting over her life she wrote: "I think these difficult times have helped me to understand better than before how infinitely rich and beautiful life is in every way."

Pursue Optimism

Jesus said that if we seek, we will find. If we ask, we will receive. If we knock, the door will open (Matthew 7:8). The Bible also says, you don't have because you don't ask (James 4:2).

Many times we don't experience health and healing because we don't intentionally pursue it. We wait for it to come to us, and then grow angry or depressed when it doesn't arrive in a timely manner.

Seek what is good and positive.

Chase it down.

Don't let it escape.

The root of the word "optimism" involves focusing on the best. What, then, is an optimist? This is an individual who embraces the following practices.

See the Best

In other words, we look for the good in every person we meet and every situation we face. We are surrounded by beauty and goodness. Distracted as we are by the negatives of life, most of us don't see it. Yes, there are certainly plenty of bad and hurtful things in this fallen world of ours, but there are also wonders, miracles, and great beauty. How sad if we allow ourselves to become so overwhelmed by the bad things that we're blinded to the good things!

Believe the Best

If we anticipate the best, there's a chance it will happen. This is the core of faith. As Pamela Reeve writes: "Faith is…reliance on the certainty that God has a pattern for my life when everything seems meaningless." Faith believes that God is in control and that His ways are good. Believing the best allows us to see the best.

Choose the Best

Optimism is ultimately a choice. We can choose to reject or embrace it. Our contentment is not based upon our circumstances; it is based upon our choices. As for me, I choose to be positive and optimistic. I choose laughter and fun. I choose joy and hope. I choose life, and I choose to live it to the fullest.

Live the Best

To live the best involves walking in faith and trusting God. As David sang, "My soul finds rest in God alone" (Psalm 62:1). Living close to God is the best there can be, for He promises us joy, peace, strength, hope, and comfort. What could be better? God will make your life shine. As Mary Gardiner Brainard insisted, "I would rather walk with God in the dark than go alone in the light."

Optimism can be learned and developed, pursued and embraced. And in so doing we will find the truth and reality of David's prayer: "You have made known to me the path of life; you will fill me with joy in your presence, with eternal pleasures at your right hand" (Psalm 16:11).

Thank God for Growth

Rejoicing in all that is good, a thankful heart can't help but smile. Mother Teresa, in the midst of all the pain and suffering in the poorest back alleys of India, said, "The best way to show my gratitude to God is to accept everything, even my problems, with joy."

Gratitude lifts us above the negativity and mediocrity of life. It energizes us and excites us and infuses us with joy.

If each day we reviewed all we have to be thankful for, it would soon change our attitude. Thankfulness flows from a daily awareness of God's hand on our shoulder. The suffering may be hard, but His tender mercies are real. With this awareness, we can join the apostle Paul "and always be thankful" (Colossians 3:15, NLT).

It's easy to thank God for the good times, but it's much more important to thank Him for the difficult times. It is through our wounds that we grow. Thanking God for them moves us forward and brightens our perspective. An optimist has learned the joy of thankfulness. Once we are thankful, we know we have overcome the darkness of our wounds.

The Transformation

123

Stormie's life was horrible. She was a victim, but she didn't stay that way. She chose to look up instead of looking back. She decided to cry out to God, and He taught her the art of overcoming. King David writes of this process of transformation by sharing his heart. "I waited patiently for the LORD to help me, and he turned to me and heard my cry. He lifted me out of the pit of despair, out of the mud and the mire. He set my feet on solid ground and steadied me as I walked along. He has given me a new song to sing" (Psalm 40:1-3, NLT).

God gave Stormie a new song.

He wants to give us a new song, too. All we have to do is be willing to sing it. That's what overcoming is all about. That's optimism. That's the joy of transformation.

1. In what ways has a negative attitude kept you from healing as fast as you wish?

2. When do you tend to be the most negative?

   when angry   when ignored
   when lonely   when stressed
   when embarrassed   when discouraged
   when hungry   when tired
   when things seem   when overlooked
     unfair

3. List three things for which you are thankful. Share them with a friend and thank God for how He has blessed you, even when things are truly tough.

4. Try your best to be positive and optimistic to the next person you meet. Notice how he or she responds to you—and how this makes you feel.

Darkness and Land Mines

[Steve]

When it's dark, look for the stars.

Robert Schuller

isa hated her life!

All the other teenagers could run and play and eat whatever they wanted. Yet because of chronic fatigue syndrome and diabetes, Lisa was so exhausted she slept up to eighteen hours a day and had to carefully screen everything that went into her mouth.

Angry and depressed, Lisa told her family how miserable she was. Life was unfair, and at various times she blamed her parents, her doctors, her friends, and even God.

Over the next few years her physical conditions improved, but her attitude didn't. She had grown bitter and negative. Everything in her life had to be perfect and she had to be in control. She didn't trust anybody. Lisa pushed everybody away and then complained how selfish people were for not being her friends.

"If God hadn't given me a defective body, I wouldn't be so miserable," she said.

"Lisa, you have managed your medical problems," I told her. "That's not what is making you miserable. Not now. It's your attitude."

Wounds create pain and darkness, but the pain can be eased and the darkness can be chased away by the light. Yet each wound plants five potential land mines in our life. These bombs can do great damage to our heart. They can explode in our face, destroy our positive attitude, and rip our life apart. They can cripple us without warning, leaving us more wounded than we began. We must search our emotional and intellectual world to remove these dangers.

Lisa's wounds made her life difficult, but what hurt her most were the land mines she stepped on. These bombs can be avoided or defused and their damage reversed, but we have to be willing.

As I spoke to Lisa, it was clear that she had survived her wounds, but the mental land mines were killing her. Let's look at five attitudes that can blow up the progress we have made and keep our wounds fresh and raw.

Land Mine #1: Comparison

There will always be someone who has it easier or looks better or was blessed in some way that we weren't. Somebody always has something better, newer, or more attractive. And when we are wounded, *everybody* seems happier and stronger. The more we compare, the less satisfied we feel.

Comparisons only make us feel more inadequate. They steal our energy, undermine our morale, and place one more weight on shoulders already bent and burdened.

The truth is, we are all unique—each with both amazing strengths and frustrating weaknesses. The first of three problems with comparison is that we usually compare our weakness with another's strength—leading us to a skewed apples/oranges conclusion. Second, what we believe we see in someone else might not be reality! We tend to exaggerate and overestimate the strengths of others. Finally—and please hear this—*our wounds and weaknesses, though painful, carry secret treasures and strengths that could be gained no other way.* Our wounds do not make us inferior, but too often they cause us to feel inferior.

Comparisons accomplish nothing positive.

In the church at Corinth, the apostle Paul found himself dealing with a whole clique of comparison junkies. In his letter to that church, Paul asserted, "When they measure themselves by themselves and compare themselves with themselves, they are not wise" (2 Corinthians 10:12).

God made us who we are, and He remains intimately aware of our circumstances—down to the tiniest detail. No matter what our difficulty, He will guide us and walk with us on life's pathway. David wrote: "Every day of my life was recorded in your book. Every moment was laid out." (Psalm 139:16, NLT). To compare is to say, "God, I think

127

You messed up here." We are each valued in His eyes, and our wounds (if you can receive this now) *increase* our value.

SEVEN THINGS TO AVOID COMPARING

Circumstances: What happens to others

Opportunities: What advantages others have

Mistakes: What errors others make

Pain: How deeply others are suffering

Abilities: What strengths others possess

Reasons: The causes of others' wounds

Emotions: How well others manage their feelings

Even if we don't compare, we are frequently surrounded by those who do. We may feel as if people are constantly comparing us to others. Many of these feelings are based in our insecurity, fear, and paranoia. Yet there are times we are really being compared. People like to pigeonhole, comparing individuals with one another. It's neither right nor fair nor healthy, but that doesn't stop them. When we are already wounded, we usually feel as if we're on the negative end of these comparisons.

But these people don't know the whole story, do they? In fact, most of the time they don't know very much at all. They don't have all the facts, and they haven't walked in our shoes. God, however, does have all the facts. And in a sense, Jesus has been in our shoes—when He became a man and walked the dusty back roads of planet earth. God doesn't compare. He is a wiser Father than that. He accepts and loves us for who we are, wounds, weaknesses, and all.

Land Mine #2: Complaining

Life rarely unfolds the way we wish, hope, or imagine. Reality has a way of deflating our highly inflated dreams. And what happens when things go wrong (as they inevitably will)?

Sometimes we complain.

We often feel cheated, ripped off, or mistreated. Deep in our heart we expect things to go our way. We expect life to be easy (or at least *easier than this!*). In those times, our disappointment tends to spill over through our lips.

When we've been wounded, it's easy to feel we're entitled to some special treatment. Special handling. Maybe like the world owes us something. Since we have suffered, we may believe that we deserve something good to compensate for all the bad. People should treat us with more care or compassion. They should give us a break. They shouldn't expect as much out of us.

If we don't get what we think we're entitled to, we complain.

What a snare this attitude can become to us! The plain, unvarnished truth is that, wounded or not, *we aren't entitled to anything*. That statement may fly in the face of political correctness, but it is absolutely true. Life is a gift, and all that is good is a gift. Entitlement is a false and selfish reality—a narrow pathway that plunges steeply into bitterness.

Besides that, complaining is simply unattractive.

You might even say ugly.

It promotes negativity, self-pity, unhappiness, and discord. Helen Keller wrote that complaints cloud the mind. Problems don't lead to complaining, but complaining frequently leads to problems. Rather than feeling better about "venting," the complainer feels worse—and life's difficulties begin to look more overwhelming than they really are.

Let's face it, there will always be something to complain about. But maturity knows how to stay silent when life doesn't go well. It knows that life is full of hurts and frustrations, but that complaints keep us focused on the problems rather than the solutions. Anthony J. D'Angelo wrote, "If you have time to whine and complain about something, then you have the time to do something about it."

Complaining keeps us from moving forward and reclaiming our emotional and spiritual health. It ignores what we have and reminds us of what we lack. It keeps us wounded and traps us into feeling sorry for ourselves. To grow we must follow the apostle Paul's direction: "Do everything without complaining" (Philippians 2:14).

Land Mine #3: Criticism

Criticism is the ugly stepsister of complaining. If complaining makes us unhappy and negative, then criticism makes us miserable and bitter. Criticism tears down. It looks for what's wrong and gets so focused on that wrong that anything right or good or positive is minimized. The critic exaggerates a small shadow until it looms so large that she can no longer see the sun. A critical spirit hardens our heart, deepens our wound, and pushes people away. An old proverb says: "The one who is critical walks alone."

Criticism is a boomerang—whatever we throw out will ultimately return to us. Another way of saying it is: "Those who criticize will be criticized." *Even if the criticism is accurate, it rarely accomplishes anything good.* We usually criticize for one of the following four reasons:

- ☀ *To show disapproval:* We don't like something or it doesn't seem fair, so we want the world to know our opinion.

- ☀ *To place blame:* We don't want anybody to be angry at us or think less of us, so we blame someone else.

- ☀ *To feel better:* We feel inferior or insecure, so we find fault with others so we don't look as bad.

- ☀ *To gain power:* We feel powerless or out of control, so we try to appear as if we know more or are superior.

No matter what our motive for criticizing others, it never gets us what we really want. If we show our disapproval, people see us as petty. If we place blame, people believe we're judgmental. If we try to feel better, people consider us selfish or shallow. If we seek to gain power, people consider us arrogant. A critical spirit will stunt and blight the growth of a healthy attitude.

The opposite of criticism is praise, or encouragement. If we have been generous with our criticism and stingy with our praise, then our very happiness and health will require us to turn that situation on its head. Paul writes: "So encourage each other and build each other up" (1 Thessalonians 5:11, NLT). In so doing, we become stronger and healthier.

It's hard to even describe what an impact this truth can have in our own home under our own roof. The Bible says, "A wise woman builds her house; a foolish woman tears hers down with her own hands" (Proverbs 14:1, NLT). Please hear this: *Nothing* tears down a marriage or family like criticism, and *nothing* builds and restores it like words of encouragement and praise.

H. Jackson Brown Jr. provides wise advise when he says: "Let the refining and improving of your own life keep you so busy that you have little time to criticize others."

Land Mine #4: Cynicism

Cynical people make me weep. So sad and miserable that they rarely smile, these unhappy women and men become blind to joy or beauty or wonder—even when it's right before their eyes.

Cynicism is a form of suicide—a slow, painful, and totally avoidable form of death. This is an individual who holds so tightly to her own wounds that they become poisoned. The resulting bitterness, like an aggressive cancer, grows and expands until it takes over every aspect of who we are—emotionally, intellectually, socially, spiritually, and even physically.

CYNICAL PEOPLE SEE LIFE AS:

- pessimistic
- hopeless
- painful
- unfair
- frightening
- negative
- depressing
- cruel
- threatening
- disappointing
- dangerous
- evil

Renee was sexually abused by her father. Her college boyfriend was unfaithful. After one year of marriage, she came home to find her husband in bed with her best friend. Renee was shattered. Ten years later her wound has turned bitter. She hates men and doesn't trust anyone. She is thirty-two but looks fifty. She wears a constant frown, and her words cut like a blade. When I asked her what might make things better, she replied with: "Men are pigs and God hates me. Life is a joke. It starts out bad and every day it gets worse. Nothing can make things better."

Renee is wrong.

Things can get better.

But if a woman gets stuck in a rut of comparison, complaining, and criticism, sooner or later cynicism will grow like mold in a damp basement. To the cynic, everything is a problem with no achievable solution. Small problems loom as insurmountable obstacles. Everything appears bad. And changes? Why, they'll only make things worse! Everybody is incompetent, dangerous, or a personal threat of some sort.

Cynicism is a poison, and even a little bit of it can make you sick. Paul tells us to "get rid of all bitterness" (Ephesians 4:31, NLT) because he knew that bitterness is the root of cynicism.

Like a good physician, however, the apostle not only identifies our symptoms and diseases, he also prescribes good medicine. In his letter to the Philippians, he writes: "Fix your thoughts on what is true and honorable and right. Think about things that are pure and lovely and admirable. Think about things that are excellent and worthy of praise" (Philippians 4:8, NLT).

Remember…with God there is *always* hope.

Land Mine #5: Compulsivity

Many wounded women cover their wounds with perfectionism. "When I feel overwhelmed, I've got to clean," said Sarah. "It helps me feel in control if I can get everything perfect and in order."

If we can make everything appear perfect, it distracts us from our inner pain. We compulsively work on polishing the surface of life so the broken and imperfect core doesn't show through. In many ways this is the opposite of cynicism, which sees everything as negative and has given up. Compulsivity is driven to make everything not just positive, but *perfect.* It refuses to give up. In every comparison, it strives to be the best. Its complaining or criticism is not aimed toward others; it's aimed toward oneself. Nothing one does is good enough unless it's perfect.

The goals of compulsive behavior are simple.

Simple and impossible.

- Perfect grades
- Perfect composure
- Perfect body
- Perfect attitude
- Perfect performance
- Perfect family
- Perfect house

The compulsive woman believes she has failed if everything is not "just right." She is easily disappointed because things rarely turn out as well as she would like. Much of this compulsivity and perfectionism is based upon fear.

1. Fear of rejection

2. Fear of failure

3. Fear of being found out

4. Fear of disappointing others

These fears keep us driven toward the unattainable and set us up for failure. Here are a few ways to avoid this land mine.

Admit that perfectionism is impossible

No one is perfect, and nothing we do will be perfect. "Perfect Tens" don't exist anywhere outside of Hollywood fantasy. We are wounded, and that's reality. The more we try to cover up that wound, the more frustrated, exhausted, and defeated we will feel. Besides, perfectionists make most of us nervous. They don't seem real, and we can't relate to them. And who can relax and kick back in a house where the couch cushions have no wrinkles, everything is perfectly in place, and not even a speck of dust rests on a single surface?

Give ourselves permission to make mistakes

We must all accept that mistakes and stumbles are a part of life. Making a mistake does not mean we are a failure. Expectations for a mistake-free life are unrealistic...absurd. We all make mistakes every day. Rather than flailing ourselves, we can all challenge ourselves to do a little better tomorrow than we did yesterday.

Accept our strengths and weaknesses

We all have areas that we excel in and areas in which we inevitably fall flat on our face. We don't need to pretend we have it all together, because we don't and we never will. *But that's okay.* We can celebrate our strengths and lean on others to help us cope with those irritating and sometimes embarrassing weaknesses.

Recognize that our wounds create limitations

Wounds leave scars. Wounds create limps. Certain things would be easier if our hurts had never happened. To act as if our wounds are irrelevant is foolish. Yet to give up as a result of them is equally foolish. In most situations there are specific things we can do to minimize the limitations our wounds bring. But the healthy choice is to swallow our pride and seek help from friends, pastors, counselors, organizations, books…or from wherever our compassionate Lord might be directing us for help.

Do our realistic best

Doing things well is important. But there is nothing more discouraging than attempting to do what can't be done. While a perfect job is impossible, most of us can do a *good* job if we put in the time and effort. As a counselor (and a friend), I encourage people to do the best they can without putting themselves down for falling short of perfection.

Defusing the Land Mines

Don't minimize these five lethal land mines! Triggering them can unleash deadly negative force, blasting and shattering hopes of healing and happiness, imprisoning people behind iron bars of bitterness.

Ironically, it is rarely our wounds that cripple or destroy us. It is the aftermath—it is how we *handle* the land mines that can have that deadly potential. If we are intentional, we can step around them. If we are careful, we can even defuse them.

The existence of land mines does not mean there must be an explosion. Yet it does mean that we must keep our eyes wide open and guard our hearts. Solomon gave us a similar warning when he wrote, "Above all else, guard your heart, for it affects everything you do" (Proverbs 4:23, NLT).

Amy Carmichael was born in northern Ireland in 1867. At an early age she felt called to help the poor, and in spite of struggles with her health, this feeling grew more compelling with age. When she was twenty-eight, she packed up and moved to Dohnavur, in southern India. Here she saved over a thousand children from horrific lives as temple prostitutes.

One day, as Amy was praying, she felt that God was preparing her for some sort of expanded impact. So she prayed, "God use me in a greater way so Thy will may come to pass." The next day she fell, breaking her leg and injuring her spine. For the rest of her life, Amy was confined to her bed. Yet instead of comparing or complaining or becoming cynical, Amy saw this as a new opportunity.

During the next twenty years, Amy Carmichael had much more time to write, penning some of her most powerful and influential books. These works spread her impact beyond India and beyond her lifetime. In the midst of this painful confinement she wrote: "Let us not be surprised when we have to face difficulties. When the wind blows hard on a tree, the roots stretch and grow the stronger. Let it be so with us."

We cannot control most of the wounds that mark our lives, but we can defuse the land mines that surround them. A healthy person can have no part of comparisons, complaining, criticism, cynicism, or compulsion. These only exaggerate our wounds and increase our limitations. So push away the dark clouds and defuse the land mines. In so doing, we learn the truth in the words of John Wooden: "Things turn out best for the people who make the best of the way things turn out."

139

1. With whom do you compare yourself? How does this make you feel?

2. On a scale of 1 to 10 (with ten being the maximum), how critical are you of yourself and others? How does this impact your healing and forward movement in life?

3. Which of the following fears tend to push you toward perfectionism: fear of rejection, fear of failure, fear of being found out, and/or fear of disappointing others?

4. Ask a friend to consider your life and name three positive qualities. Embrace these strengths and thank God for them.

Embraced by God's Healing Presence

[Pam]

> More spiritual progress can be made in one short
> moment of speechless silence in the awesome
> presence of God than in years of mere study.
>
> A. W. Tozer

We aren't wired to bear our burdens alone. Our heavenly Father never intended for us to heal from our wounds without His help. This is the God who knows all the details of the heartache we've endured, and seeks to be our Comforter.

The word *comfort* literally means "to call near."

What a beautiful picture!

Think of one person calling out to another to come stand alongside him or her. It indicates what God does when we cry out in our pain and sorrow to Him and invite Him into our troubled state.

Everything about God is relational. He is always with us. We also learn from God's love letters, the Bible, that God is especially tender toward those with broken hearts. David, who was viciously mistreated and abused in the years of his young manhood, wrote, "The LORD is close to the brokenhearted; he rescues those who are crushed in spirit" (Psalm 34:18, NLT).

The psalmist declares a God who "heals the broken-hearted, binding up their wounds," adding that "the LORD's delight is in those who honor him, those who put their hope in his unfailing love" (Psalm 147:3, 11, NLT).

Even though we may believe God is with us, sometimes it's a struggle to sense His presence—particularly when we experience a dark night of the soul. Pain has a way of blunting our awareness of God's nearness—just when we need that assurance the most. In our efforts to cope, we can become so preoccupied with the human realm—what we see, taste, touch, feel, and hear—that we lose sight of the spirit realm. We forget that the very essence of who we are is spirit.

God has resources to meet our needs that can only be accessed in and through His Spirit. It's safe to say that many times we don't experience God's provision because we don't tap into His supply line. Instead, we act as if we have to make our own way and our healing is all up to us. We recoil in our pain, pulling away from others and from God. In our self-reliance we assume that if we hold to a list of dos and don'ts and execute the right combination of self-help strategies, then things will get better.

I suppose this is one way to approach recovery.

But not a very good one.

In my personal and professional experience, this sort of attitude can end up prolonging and complicating the healing process. Recovery efforts apart from God's healing grace typically deliver less than satisfying results.

Through my twenty-five years of clinical practice, time and again I've witnessed the Spirit of God orchestrate breakthroughs in clients' lives. These interventions went beyond the clinical tools I offered, and beyond my clients' abilities to make wise choices.

The breakthroughs were *supernatural*. That's the only way I can explain it. They came as wounded women spent time alone with God, crying out to Him in their pain, praying for wisdom and insight, reading His Word, and asking Him to do the impossible.

And He has. Again and again and again.

In my own personal seasons of suffering, it has been my interactions with God that have accelerated more healing than anything else. Significant exchanges occurred between my spirit and God's Spirit when we met together. Healing came as I purged tension from my body and soul through prayer walks. It came through reading His Word and taking time to listen to what God said to me as we fellowshipped together in my darkness. It came as He realigned my feelings with my faith. Had I not intentionally and regularly opened my heart to the Spirit of God, I'd probably still be immobilized by overwhelming sadness and fear.

How can we expose our wounds to God's restoring touch? That's an important question for any of us to ask. How can I position myself to be embraced by His healing presence? Through the years I've discovered some answers that have made all the difference in the world.

Call on God

When life delivers a sequence of devastating blows that leave us reeling in agony, it's hard to even think straight, much less institute a ten-step formula found in a recovery book. In the midst of tragedy we instinctively cry out from the depths of our anguish, *"Oh God…HELP me!"*

Even people who claim no religious affiliation tend to call on God in desperate times. I refer to this as spiritual instinct. No matter how we have conditioned our mind, our spirit *knows* we need to connect with God's Spirit. When we have tapped out our own resources and our self-reliance fails us, we intuitively know we need to reach for help beyond ourselves. God is acutely aware of our afflictions and makes this bold promise to us: "'If you look for me in earnest, you will find me when you seek me. I will be found by you,' says the LORD" (Jeremiah 29:13–14, NLT).

Notice the specific wording of this promise. Through the prophet Jeremiah, God says, "When you seek Me, you will find Me." In other words: "The answers to the nagging life questions that keep you awake at night…*are in Me.* The consolations that can penetrate the core of your pain and bring a settled peace that passes understanding...*are in Me.* The divine perspectives that can radically alter your outlook, clear confusion, realign your spirit, change your disposition, and create deep, long-lasting healing...*are in Me, and Me alone.*"

When we are wounded, we have choices. We can obsessively look within and be consumed by our conflicts, or we can cry out to God, asking Him to embrace us with His healing presence and to be who we need Him to be in the moment. At the first hint of our call, He comes to our aid.

God knows our frailties and how cruel this world can be. He knows when we are fragile in body and soul. When our world is shattered and we're so overwhelmed we don't even know how to pray, He says to us, "I'm here to help. I'm pleading for you. Come to Me and let Me heal your broken heart."

God is not silent. He responds to the heart cry of His people. It doesn't matter how we format our cries. They can be long hard sighs; deep, guttural groans; a single word shot toward heaven; or ongoing paragraphs with run-on sentences. He hears, and steps into our lives to make a difference.

David, who endured some dreadful wounds of his own, speaks of God's faithfulness to hear and respond: "My heart is in anguish. The terror of death overpowers me. Fear and trembling overwhelm me. I can't stop shaking.... But I will call on God, and the LORD will rescue me. Morning, noon, and night I plead aloud in my distress, and the LORD hears my voice. He rescues me and keeps me safe from the battle waged against me, even though many still oppose me…. Give your burdens to the LORD, and he will take care of you." (Psalm 55:4–5, 16–18, 22, NLT).

David says, "I will call on God, and He will rescue."

Our job is to call. God's job is to rescue.

Our job is to cry out. His job is to orchestrate the results.

The Lord reminded me of this division of labor recently in a kind but confrontational way. I happened to be very burdened about a situation. During a quiet moment I wrote in my prayer journal: "God, what do You want me to do?"

I sensed God answer: *"Cross out the* me.*"*

A bit confused I asked, "Cross out the *me*?"

"Yes, cross out the me.*"*

I'm a little slow at times, but after some reflection, I finally got it. He wanted me to cross out the word "me" in the question I had just written. When I did, the question looked like this: "God, what do You want to do?"

The Spirit of God flipped on the light in my darkness and showed me I was asking the wrong question. My focus was in the wrong direction. Instead, God wanted me to ask: "What do You want to do in this situation?"

I shook my head in amusement over how gently and creatively God had pinpointed my tendency toward self-reliance. Following the Spirit's lead, I asked the better question. His response eased my burden: *"I want to show you My goodness."*

God never ceases to speak to us, but the noise of the world without and the tumult of our passions within bewilder us and prevent us from listening to Him.

—FRANCOIS FENELON

Take Time to Listen

A journal can be a valuable tool for meeting with God and letting go of our heartache. If you've never tried journaling, you might be surprised how much it helps. Don't think "diary" here. This is a record of our thoughts, prayers, and the specific things we've sensed that God's Spirit has spoken into our lives. Sitting down to write our jumbled thoughts and emotions, we begin to diffuse our pent-up tension. Seeing our feelings in black and white on the paper in front of us brings clarity and helps us understand what's going on inside.

I like to journal my thoughts and feelings in the form of prayers. I give God an earful, and then I listen. He offers a strong invitation to all of us. He says, "Listen, and I will tell you where to get food that is good for the soul! Come to me with your ears wide open. Listen, for the life of your soul is at stake" (Isaiah 55:2–3, NLT).

Through the years, I've discovered the essential thing is not so much what I say to God, but what God says to me. Sometimes what God speaks to my spirit may offend my mind because it doesn't fit my logic or assumptions. Nevertheless, whatever He speaks promotes health. Even when the truth hurts, it heals.

147

One afternoon, grieving some recent losses and feeling gripped by fear about the future, I wrote in my journal: "God, I *hate* being in this place. It's dark and scary...." I wrote several more paragraphs and then finished my thoughts with, "And on top of all that, I am sick of grieving!"

Relief came as I honestly expressed my feelings without censorship. After placing the period at the end of my last sentence, these words passed through my mind: *I don't want you to grieve; I want you to trust.*

That idea hit me like a two-by-four between the eyes. The Holy Spirit was giving me an assignment that seemed to contradict my clinical training and former life experience. After all, it's normal to grieve when we've lost something near and dear to us. But in the quiet of the moment, I knew my Father's voice, and His words were life to my soul. I've learned that there are times when God's directives don't line up with human reasoning, and that I had best pay attention to what God is saying because it's always for my highest good.

In the months that followed that encounter, I made a concerted effort to take a stance of trust, particularly when my heartache was more severe. On the days I felt like I was drowning in waves of sadness, I wrote in my journal: "Trust God, Pam.... Trust God.... He will do what He said He will do.... He will do what you cannot do.... Just trust Him."

It's more obvious to me now, years later, that these Spirit-driven words both promoted healing and protected me from falling into a bottomless pit of self-pity and depression.

It pays to take time to listen. We can listen anytime, and in any place, because God is with us twenty-four hours a day, eagerly waiting for a listening ear. Some of my best conversations with Him have occurred as I've walked through surrounding neighborhoods, pushing the tension out of my body and the troubles out of my soul.

Push the Tension Out

I'll admit it. I'm an addict. I'm hooked on power walking and addicted to praying and watching God answer.

Had it not been for the prayer support of my walking buddies during my darker years, I might have lost my sanity. Each week our cross trainers beat the pavement and our prayers bombarded heaven. I prayed. My friends prayed. Back and forth we talked out loud to God, asking for divine interventions on behalf of the people and situations that concerned us. Relief came from pushing the tension out of our bodies while pursuing God.

I remember one afternoon when I was praying along our five-mile loop, tied up in knots over my daughter. Her recovery was happening about as fast as a slug creeping across the warm pavement on a summer day. As I walked, God got an earful: "God, I feel so helpless. I'm not seeing much change, and I don't know how to help. Am I doing too little? Am I doing too much? Show me, God, what I need to do."

Instantly a picture flashed onto the screen of my mind. I saw a huge toolbox brimming over with hundreds of tools. (I'm a visual learner, and sometimes God gets my attention best with pictures.) I sensed God saying, *"Pam, you are simply one tool that I'm using to shape her life."*

In my confusion, I had asked a question. God's response addressed my deeper need. He knew I was trying to carry too much of the weighty responsibility for Jessie's well-being. He reminded me that He is God. Her healing was up to Him, not me, and I was simply one person He was using in the process. God was prompting me to place Jessie back in His hands (for the umpteenth time) and to trust Him again.

In complete abandonment I cried out to Him:

Okay, God. I understand what You are saying to me…the healing I long for in Jessie's life isn't up to me. The assignment is too big for me. But it's not too big for You! You are Jessie's God, and You are at work in her life. You have promised me that the good work You began in her You will finish. What You initiate, You complete. I see now that I'm simply one of many tools You are using. I surrender to You, to Your plan, to Your timing, and to Your outcome. I believe You are a miracle-working God. Once again I place Jessie in Your loving hands, trusting You to be her God…to be our God, and to astound us with Your goodness…

Looking back (isn't hindsight amazing?), I can clearly see that the more I trusted God, the more trustworthy I found Him. The harder I leaned on Him, the more support He supplied. It wasn't trust, in and of itself, that brought me peace. It was the One in whom I trusted. As I took time to be quiet, He heightened my awareness of His unseen, undeniable presence.

I came to experience Him as my Peace.

The more I sensed His nearness, the easier it was for me to let go of self-reliance. The more I focused on God's capability, the less overwhelmed I felt by my inabilities. The more I reminded myself of God's sovereign power, the less intimidated I was by the things I couldn't control. In all this, I was forcing my feelings into the backseat, riding behind my faith.

151

Declare Your Faith

Shortly after Nathan's difficult entry into this world, I developed an acrostic for the word FAITH. I used it as a helpful reminder of what I needed to do when I was scared about the future and overwhelmed with the realities before us.

FAITH:
Fully
Abandoned to God
In
Trust and
Humility

When we've been wounded, we find ourselves vulnerable to those gnawing "what ifs." We need to tilt our head heavenward, raise our hands in surrender, and say, "God, no matter what, I am fully abandoned to You in trust and humility." It is this posture of faith that positions us to receive whatever we need from God.

When we are suffering hardship or emerging from the shadows of a dark time in our lives, our confidence is shaken. Wounds break down our psychological defenses and often create faith crises. We find ourselves asking questions that would be unthinkable during happier seasons of life:

- ⊛ Where is God?

- ⊛ Does God love me?

- ⊛ Why did this happen?

- ⊛ Can anything good possibly come out of something so bad?

Our emotional confusion can distort our spiritual perception. Coping with the pain of our wounds requires a tremendous amount of mental energy. If you have recently suffered a wound, please give yourself grace. Give yourself time to process the pain, and position yourself to receive from God what you need to restore your bearings. Ask God to give you a spirit of faith that will enable you to fully abandon yourself to Him in trust and humility.

As we heal from our wounds, there will be times when

our emotions will strive to dictate our choices and drive discouragement. We must remember that faith and feelings are not the same thing. We can be steadfast in our faith regardless of what our emotions are saying. Rather than allowing our emotions to rule, we can dethrone them with the truth of God's Word. We simply proclaim what God says is fact when we are hurting. This forces our soul to yield to our spirit and our feelings to submit to our faith. I hope some of my favorite faith statements will inspire you to make your own list…and that you'll discover the joy that comes when the truth sets you free.

Faith vs. Feelings

153

Through the years I've strengthened my faith using reminders like these….

When your **feelings** say, "God has left you. He doesn't care. You're on your own"…

…**Faith** says, "In God's kingdom everything is based on promise, not on feeling."

When your **feelings** say, "People will rip you off. Don't trust them"…

…**Faith** says, "God is my Redeemer. He will return whatever is stolen, one way or another."

When your **feelings** say, "You've blown it. Everyone is talking. Your reputation is smeared for life"…

...**Faith** says, "God will straighten the record when false things have been said about me."

When your **feelings** say, "You're going to be on hold forever"...

...**Faith** says, "My time is in God's hands. His plans for me will be accomplished right on schedule."

When your **feelings** say, "If God really loved you, He would give you what you want"...

...**Faith** says, "God always acts for my highest good."

When your **feelings** say, "You can't trust God. Look how He has let you down"...

...**Faith** says, "God has proven His trustworthiness by sending His Son to die on the cross for me."

When your **feelings** say, "Your scars will limit you for life"...

...**Faith** says, "I am useful to God not in spite of my scars, but because of them."

Our wounds, grievous and difficult to bear as they may be, do not have to define us or determine our future. Instead, they can become an opportunity to experience God's healing presence, launching us into a deeper understanding of the interactive ways of His Spirit. Malcolm Muggeridge reminds us, "The Comforter needs only to be summoned. The need is the call, the call is the presence, and the presence is the Comforter, the Spirit of Truth."

Remember, everything about God is relational. As we

commune with Him in our pain, exchanges take place. Our spirit connects with His Spirit, and the essence of who He is renews us. In the fractured places of our lives, we trade our pain for His provision. We come to know Him as the One who sustains and heals the brokenhearted. As we persist in His presence, the Spirit speaks truth to our spirit, radically altering our perceptions, settling our emotions, and transforming us from the inside out.

God's answer to our pain is always, "Come to Me."

He is the Wonderful Counselor, like no other.

And when you come to Him as the Wonderful Counselor, when you feel His arms around you, you will know your God by yet another name.

Prince of Peace.

1. Under what circumstances are you most likely to call on God?

2. When you talk to God, how do you expect Him to respond to you?

3. In what ways does God tend to lead you?

   through circumstances   through passion
   through people   through common sense
   through a "still, small   through Scripture
      voice"   through dreams
   through peace in your   through images
      heart   through words

4. Find a quiet place in your home, backyard, or local park where you can enjoy solitude. Take thirty minutes to be silent and ask God to speak to you. If you feel stuck, try one of the following:

   ❀ sing a worship song

   ❀ focus on God's handiwork in nature

   ❀ read a passage of Scripture and expect God to meet with you

The Comfort of Caring People

[Steve]

Oh, the comfort, the inexpressible comfort
of feeling safe with a person....

DINAH MARIA MULOCK CRAIK

was lonely, guilty, dirty, full of fear," writes Lee Ezell in her autobiography, *The Missing Piece*.

Lee had been raped, was pregnant, and found herself alone and friendless in a strange city. Confused and desperate, this eighteen-year-old met Mom and Dad Croft at a local church.

When Mom Croft learned of Lee's condition, she said, "Now don't you worry about a thing. Mom Croft's going to take care of you. We'll fix you a place to sleep at our house, and you just stay with us until you have your baby."

And that's what happened. Lee moved into the Croft's home where she was loved, accepted, and cared for. Years later she wrote: "The Crofts were modern-day

Good Samaritans. They really didn't have room for me in their home, but they made room anyway.... They had the rare gift of generosity, for their world was so big that there was always room for those who were in need or unwanted by others.... Here I was at peace for the first time in many months."

Because Lee was able to reach out to people, they reached out to her.

If Lee had totally isolated, drawing herself into a protective cocoon, if she had never sought connection with others in that local church, life might have been very, very different for her. And infinitely more difficult. She would have never encountered a loving older couple who became like parents to her, and she would have had to face her wounds and hardships alone.

In the years that followed, she had a successful marriage and became a popular writer, speaker, and radio personality.

But Lee Ezell has never, never forgotten that when life is the hardest, we need people the most.

When we are wounded, we feel disconnected from people. Sometimes we even want to run away and hide. Though we secretly yearn for people, we don't feel safe with them. We're afraid they will hurt us more. We feel vulnerable, broken, inferior, hypervigilant, and insecure.

But mostly, we're just scared.

Though people have hurt us in the past and will probably hurt us again, we still need them. People-contact is crucial to our healing and health. To grow, we need to learn to trust again by reaching out to others…and allowing them to reach out to us.

Still unconvinced? Here are six ways we need people.

1. Keeping Us Company

"Loneliness," wrote Norman Vincent Peale, "lurks in the shadows of adversity." When we are lonely, we feel deserted, abandoned, and secluded. We feel isolated and wonder if "anyone out there" wants to spend time with us. Ironically, when we are wounded we may build walls, keeping others at a distance—even while we yearn with all our hearts for company.

We need people to help us grow and stretch beyond ourselves.

We need people who will share our hopes, fears, and tears.

We need people to laugh with when life gets too serious and grim.

We need people to love and accept us so that we might learn to love and accept ourselves.

We need people to pull us out of hiding, that we might stand in the sunshine.

We need company when we've been wounded, but it needs to be *healthy* company. People can certainly help us, but they can also hurt and further wound us. Two of the greatest dangers in relationships are when we try to *push everyone away* and, conversely, when we try to *pull everyone close.*

As wounded individuals, we may become overprotective

of our feelings. Since the thought of being hurt again is almost too much to bear, we become mistrustful—or even fearful—of people who try to edge into our world. We build our walls high, seeking maximum shielding from potential pain.

At the opposite extreme, there may be times when we feel so broken and lonely that we embrace anyone who shows us even a hint of love or acceptance. We let others get too close, too soon, before we know whether they're safe, healthy, or trustworthy.

Both of these positions are dangerous. We don't need walls, but (sadly) we can't trust everyone we meet, either. We must be wise, reaching out to positive people and building positive relationships while maintaining healthy boundaries with those who may be unsafe or harmful.

Of course, while all of this counsel may *sound* logical, implementing it may prove very, very difficult for people in pain. Just thinking these things through might seem like an overwhelming obstacle at certain times of our life.

In such seasons, God wants us to simply ask Him for the necessary wisdom and let Him guide us. "*For I am overwhelmed and desperate, and you alone know which way I ought to turn*" (Psalm 142:3, TLB).

2. Caring for Us

We all have times when we crave comfort or encouragement from someone who cares. These are times when life feels it is at its lowest ebb. Our pain may be so great we want to give up. The world may seem so dark and empty and cruel that we wonder why we should continue to try. We may want to scream or cry or simply curl up into a ball and disappear.

How we long for someone to care in that moment...some kind and gentle someone who will lift us out of our fear, depression, anger, guilt, and shame. When writer Patsy Clairmont hit this point, she discovered that "hope comes as a companion; she slips her arm around your shoulder and offers to help you stumble toward change. That evening...I heard hope whisper, 'You are not alone.'"

Just today I spoke with a lady who recently weathered a deep personal crisis. "I was so lonely," she recalled. "Everybody I called wasn't there. All I wanted was someone—anyone—to tell me I'd be okay."

That's the way it is when you're in deep emotional pain. You reach out because you feel as though you'll die if you don't. Sometimes someone reaches back, and we are comforted by that contact, even if only for a moment. And at other times, we find the only One who responds is God Himself, drawing us into His embrace in a deeper way than we've known before.

Most of the time, however, it pleases the Father to dispense His hope and help through the hearts, hands, and voices of His sons and daughters. We are to "comfort and encourage each other" (1 Thessalonians 4:18, NLT), for these are two of the greatest needs of anyone who is wounded. As people apply these two ointments of grace, our heart softens and our body relaxes. Suddenly we can see beyond our wounds and hear the soft melodies of a brighter tomorrow.

Words

Comfort and encouragement come in at least three equally powerful packages. Someone's *words* can speak into our life, lifting us out of our despair, saying things like: "You are loved!" or "I believe in you" or "God will use you in great ways."

Words change lives. As Solomon wrote some three thousand years ago, "An encouraging word cheers a person up." And again, "Pleasant words are a honeycomb, sweet to the soul and healing to the bones" (Proverbs 12:25, NLT; 16:24).

Touch

A caring *touch* can calm a troubled heart and chase away the cold chill of loneliness. There are times we all need the gentleness of human touch—a firm embrace, an arm around our shoulders, a pat on the back, a hand to hold. In fact, without these we can shrivel and die.

A friend of mine who had lost his middle-aged wife to cancer after twenty-five years of marriage told me that for several months, several women in the church simply stepped into the role of "hugger" in his life. Without embarrassment, without hesitation, without words, without worrying about "appearances," these two or three women would simply embrace him for thirty seconds or so.

Of all the kind and generous things that good church did for him through those terrible months of grieving, that physical contact meant more to him than anything.

Henri Nouwen writes: "When we honestly ask ourselves which person in our lives means the most to us, we often find that it is those who, instead of giving advice, solutions, or cures, have chosen rather to share our pain and touch our wounds with a warm and tender hand."

Presence

Sometimes all we need, or can even accept, is someone's *presence*. Words can be wonderful, but they can also get in our way. Touch can be affirming, but it can also be frightening. Sometimes comfort and encouragement can come best when one simply stands beside us. A silent, reassuring presence can be among the best gifts we ever give someone. But as David Augsburger writes, "It is so much easier to tell a person what to do with his problem than to stand with him in his pain."

163

HOW TO CONNECT WITH OTHERS

1. Recognize your need.

> *When life is most difficult, you need people the most. They provide much-needed comfort, encouragement, and perspective.*

2. Take a risk.

> *It may feel awkward and frightening to connect with others. You may find a hundred reasons to hide inside yourself, but you need to reach out.*

3. *Call an old friend.*

> *You have longtime friends or relatives that you trust. Call one of them, even if you haven't spoken for a while.*

4. *Get involved.*

> *Find a cause, a church, a class, a club, or a committee where you'll be in regular contact with others. Then jump in, whether you feel like it or not. Remember, feelings follow actions.*

5. *Volunteer.*

> *Get out and volunteer to help others. Be active and be social. As you surround yourself with others, you will feel better.*

6. *Be careful of Internet relationships.*

> *A person in pain is more vulnerable than usual. Realize that online relationships can be deceptive.*

7. *Don't let yourself fall into self-pity.*

> *It's easy to feel sorry for yourself when you're hurting, but this only makes things worse.*

8. *Ask God for direction.*

> *Pray that God will bring to mind a person or opportunity to provide a positive connection.*

3. Helping Us Grow

We are most open to grow after we have hit bottom in our lives. In those moments, we realize that Band-Aid approaches and watered-down remedies simply won't cut it. Truly desperate and at our wits' end, we realize that we cannot emerge from our painful despair on our own.

Desperation makes us teachable.

We need someone with a flashlight who is willing to lead us from our darkness. The woman at the well was an outcast, trapped in a pattern of failed marriages and living with a man unable or unwilling to commit to her. Lost and lonely, rejected by the respectable people of her village, she was open to a new direction. She yearned for someone to "explain everything to us."

Standing alone at the well in the heat of the day, Jesus gently approached her and said, "If you only knew the gift God has for you...." He encouraged her and treated her with respect. Then He explained that she was looking for love in all the wrong places. He showed her that God could heal a wounded heart. He gave her hope and direction. She left with a joy and excitement that she hadn't felt in years—perhaps in her whole life (John 4:1–30).

When we are too close to our pain and problems, we frequently can't find a way out—even if it's right in front of us. This doesn't mean we're stupid or incompetent. All it means is that we are blinded by our wounds and by our pain. We need someone with a more objective perspective or greater life experience to come alongside us, take our hand, and lead us to a better place.

In a perfect world, these people would come to us.

In a perfect world, caring people would see us in desperate need and rush to our aid.

But as we all know, our world is far from perfect. Therefore, instead of expecting people to come in our need and our sorrow, we must go to them. We must seek wise, grace-filled, positive people to guide, direct, counsel, coach, teach, advise, and/or mentor us. This helps us move toward healing and protects us from inadvertently falling into further wounds. As Solomon wrote: "Plans fail for lack of counsel, but with many advisers they succeed" (Proverbs 15:22).

Ruth leaned on her mother-in-law, Naomi, when she didn't know where to go or what to do. Esther sought the council of her adopted father, Mordecai, when things got tough. Even Mary, the mother of Jesus, went to her cousin, Elizabeth, when faced with an unplanned pregnancy (Ruth 1–3; Esther 2:10–11, 19–20; Luke 1:39–56).

Don't let pride, shyness, or embarrassment keep you from getting the help you need to grow and be all God knows you can be. We all need help, and we all need to grow. When we are wounded, however, such help is nothing short of crucial. Even though it may seem elusive, even though we may not find it as readily as we hope, help is worth seeking.

Right now you may very much need the comforting, strengthening touch of another, but tomorrow *you* may be the one doing the helping. Paul speaks of the older women coming alongside the younger women, training them "to live wisely and be pure, to take care of their homes, to do good" (Titus 2:5, NLT).

There are times when we all need someone to come alongside us.

There are times when someone will need us to come alongside of them.

TRAITS OF A HEALTHY LIFE COACH

> *Builds communication skills*
> *Assists problem solving*
> *Improves relationships*
> *Encourages goal setting*
> *Challenges negative thinking*
> *Identifies self-destructive patterns*
> *Nurtures spiritual growth*
> *Promotes maturity*
> *Celebrates personal strengths and potential*
> *Strengthens character*

4. Praying for Us

When we know someone is praying for us, whether they are holding our hands or halfway across the world, it helps ease our pain. As someone prays for us, they invite God to touch us. Bruce Wilkinson writes: "Prayer is a path to God's blessing." Prayer is the solution to every problem. It places God's hand on our shoulder and tells us that He has not forgotten us. I love it when Paul tells his friend Timothy: "Night and day I constantly remember you in my prayers" (2 Timothy 1:3). What a connection! What an encouragement!

WHAT PRAYER PROVIDES

—*Protection*   *He will be our refuge.*
—*Purpose*   *He has great plans for us.*
—*Power*   *His power will fill us.*
—*Provision*   *He will meet our every need.*
—*Perspective* *He knows and sees all things.*
—*Peace*   *He promises a peace that passes all understanding.*

When someone prays with us, or for us, he or she invites God into our life. As Oswald Chambers wrote: "God comes in where my helplessness begins." We know how desperately we need God's help. Yet when the pain is great, we sometimes feel that He is distant. Our prayers seem to fall short of their goal, and our words feel like wasted breath. In times like these, we long for someone to intercede for us and plead our case. We need someone to provide that extra push of prayer to get us started. We want to cry out like David: "Please, God, rescue me! Come quickly, LORD, and help me" (Psalm 70:1, NLT). But our effort turns into meaningless mumbles. When someone else cries out, we can add our "amen," and the fog seems to clear.

Every day someone asks me directly or via a phone call to pray for them. Some people ask boldly, others with hesitation or fear. No matter how hectic or busy my day might be, I consider it a great privilege to pray with or for someone.

There is no greater power in the universe than the power of God.

There is no greater love in all of creation than the love of God.

And there is no one anywhere who cares more about the most minute details of our lives than God Himself. *This* is the One to whom we bring our wounded friends. And this is the One who will touch us in the deepest places of our pain and bring healing as others pray for us. What a mighty force! It connects us with each other and the Master of the universe. Without it we are disconnected from our hope.

So we all need to ask for prayer and uphold others with a steady, heartfelt pattern of prayer. As an old saying so aptly puts it: "Prayer is the key to the morning and the bolt at night."

5. Giving Back to Others

Sally was on her fourth marriage when I called her and asked if she would be a marriage mentor to a newlywed couple.

She laughed. "Dr. Steve, is this a joke? You know my history. Why in the world are you asking me?"

"I thought you'd be a great mentor," I told her. "You and Jake have been married twelve years, and you know first-hand the pain of failed marriages. So, tell me, Sally…what *have* you learned from your divorces?"

Sally hesitated a moment before she spoke. "Well…I've learned that you have to be committed—and not get so upset when things don't go your way. I've learned that if you don't work at it every day, it can fall apart. But if you do work at it, things will get better."

"And that's what I want you to teach this young couple."

Giving back to others gives our wounds meaning. It connects us with others as a mentor and coach, rather than a victim. When Henri Nouwen speaks of "the wounded healer," he hits on a powerful paradox that gives us all hope. For it is through our wounds that we can frequently give the most genuine and life-changing help.

I recently heard a story about a man and woman who had both lost their spouses through cancer. As the man described his loneliness and pain, the woman began to weep uncontrollably. Soon he placed his arm around her, and they wept together.

It's easy for our wounds to cause us to withdraw into isolation, self-pity, and protection. Yet this is a terrible waste of our experience. Paul wrote: "For when God comforts us, it is so that we, in turn, can be an encouragement to you" (2 Corinthians 1:6, NLT).

I think of Lisa, who works with troubled teens; Teresa, who volunteers at a woman's shelter; and Kia, who teaches classes on postabortion recovery. Why do these women do what they do? It's because they've been on the other side. But they're not only bringing encouragement and wisdom into the lives of other women and girls, they're reaping some good benefits of their own. As Flora Edwards once said, "In helping others, we shall help ourselves, for whatever good we give out completes the circle and comes back to us."

6. Needing One Another

Our wounds force us to face our need for one another. We all need someone to lean on—someone who will try to understand. We need people who will love us and whom we can love back. A world without relationships would be cold and lonely.

The poet Samuel Taylor Coleridge once wrote that "friendship is a sheltering tree." On a hot summer's day it shades us, and on a blustery winter's night it protects us from the storm. We all are strengthened by those who stand around us. Their smiles make us smile, and their encouragement keeps us from giving up. My best times are with people.

If our lives were perfect, we might become so self-sufficient and independent that we wouldn't need others. Yet we aren't perfect. Chuck Swindoll reminds us that "tucked away in a quiet corner of every life are wounds and scars. If they were not there, we would need no Physician. Nor would we need one another."

So let's not fight it; let's just admit we're all broken. Only then can we truly help each other make it through the hard times and celebrate with each other when all goes well.

1. When you are suffering, do you tend to push people away or draw people close? Why? Does this help or hinder your healing?

2. When have you felt most cared for by another person? What did they do? How did this help you?

3. Who has had the most impact in your life to help you toward growth and maturity? What did they do that left the greatest impression on you?

4. Make a list of five things you would like one or two trusted friends to pray about for you. E-mail them your list.

Triumph from Tragedy

[Steve]

There is nothing the body suffers
the soul may not profit by.

GEORGE MEREDITH

t was nothing more than a slight eye infection.

Nothing to worry about, except that the tiny infant was only six months old. But the young parents wanted to be safe, so they took Fanny to the doctor. Tragically, the doctor was poorly trained, and his remedy permanently blinded the baby. A few months later her father died, and her twenty-one-year-old mother hired herself out as a maid.

Even as a teenager, Fanny Crosby wrote about how happy she was. She considered herself blessed to be blind. She became a teacher at a school for the blind, but her true passion was helping the poor. When people asked her about her handicap, she would reply with all candor, "It was the best thing that ever happened to me."

Her lack of eyesight gave her an inner strength and

commitment to God. She once wrote: "If perfect earthly eyesight were offered me tomorrow I would not accept it. I might not have sung hymns to the praise of God if I had been distracted by the beautiful and interesting things about me."

Fanny wrote nearly nine thousand hymns in her life—including some of the most powerful and popular of all time. Hymns such as "Blessed Assurance," "Safe in the Arms of Jesus," "To God Be the Glory," and "I am Thine, O Lord" showcase her wonderful gifting.

In the course of her ninety-five years, she met with presidents, generals, and other dignitaries. Her philosophy toward difficulties and adversity can be best found in her hymns, where she wrote lines such as, "God will take care of you…through sunshine and shade" and "Bring Him your burden and you shall be blest." Fanny Crosby would insist that her greatest triumphs were the result of her greatest tragedy.

In fact, she celebrated her wounds.

In our culture of ease and comfort, we do all we can to avoid adversity. We think of hardships as some dreadful misfortune or terrible curse. We consider difficulties inconvenient at best, and catastrophic at worst.

In years past, people have been much more pragmatic about pain. They believed difficulties to be an integral, unavoidable part of life. In fact, they saw troubles as something to be embraced. Nearly two thousand years ago, the apostle James told us to welcome our wounds as opportunities (James 1:2).

There is a lesson in every adversity that often cannot be learned in any other way. In one of the great ironies of life, pain may be among God's richest gifts to us. Our trials and adversities hold powerful teachings that render our sufferings not only positive and meaningful, but necessary.

God doesn't want any experience in our lives to go to waste. For this reason, He makes sure that our wounds hold more benefits than most of us are ever aware. As James Buckman wrote, "Every trial endured and weathered in the right spirit makes a soul nobler and stronger than it was before." Those who have not experienced any adversity risk a shallow, self-absorbed life, for it is through our difficulties that we experience the most growth. Here are six of the ways adversity can help us grow.

Adversity...Develops Patience

Adversity slows us down—and sometimes even stops us dead in our tracks. In this quick-paced, move-as-fast-as-you-can world, we don't wait for anything. We race here and there, uncertain where we are going or what we want. Difficulties show us that we can't outrun life, with its fears and disappointments and challenges. They force us to wait—on time, on others, on God. They remind us that healing is usually a process, and the more we push it, the longer it takes.

Most of us are impatient. We like to see things happen quickly, and we get frustrated when the pace isn't as fast as we think it should be. We love to speed, but our wounds slam on the brakes. We can complain and stomp our feet, but…what good does that do?

Troubles set their own pace. They demand patience. For when we move too quickly, we miss much—the colors, the details, and sometimes even the essence of life. In a world where the accomplishment of a goal is emphasized more than the journey to get there, we skim and scan and skate as fast as we can, unaware of all that we have missed. Speed restricts our ability to concentrate and absorb. Patience allows us to learn incomparable lessons and gives us the time to weave those lessons into the very fabric of our life.

We have no time for patience. Words related to it like *silence*, *stillness*, *contemplation*, *calmness*, *tranquility*, and *endurance* seem to be from a bygone era. Yet it is here that we find ourselves and draw near to God.

Adversity…Increases Maturity

John Patrick said, "Pain makes man think."

He might have also added that it helps us grow up and mature. Wounds can give us depth and wisdom. We learn more from adversity than prosperity. Prosperity may be attractive, but it adds nothing positive or long lasting to who we are. It makes us shallow and sheltered. Hard times and difficult circumstances, however, plunge us to the depths of life—discovering truth, solving problems, and accepting limitations.

We live in a world where we do all we can to avoid and run away from difficulties, yet this only traps us in our immaturity. Maturity faces its problems and heartaches head-on, doing all it can to work through them with a positive attitude. Even if they can't quickly be solved—or *ever* solved—walking through this process creates personal depth that nothing can duplicate.

Maturity requires experience in coping with the challenges of life. Someone once wrote: "A smooth sea never made a skillful mariner." This person knew that rough waters season our souls. When a mother bird pushes her babies from the nest, there is an immediate crisis. Yet out of this crisis, the babies learn to fly. Without this trauma, the babies would stay in the nest and starve. Difficulties force us to face reality, stretch our wings, and see what possibilities may be open to us.

177

It is through our hard times that our maturity ripens and wisdom follows. Wise people have lived full lives, mining truth from every experience. They do not resent difficulties, seeing them as simply another source for growth. They recognize that adversity keeps you sharp, opening doors of wisdom that would otherwise remain closed for a lifetime. They have discovered an amazing pattern of life: Adversity provides wisdom, and wisdom shines a light on how to best approach adversity.

As Solomon wrote: "Happy is the person who finds wisdom and gains understanding. For the profit of wisdom is better than silver, and her wages are better than gold....

She offers you life in her right hand, and riches and honor in her left" (Proverbs 3:13–14,16, NLT).

Adversity...Teaches Compassion

When we have personally experienced the difficult things of life—fear, rejection, betrayal, shame, loneliness, hurt—we develop a gentle heart toward others in pain.

Our eyes have been opened to the hurts of life...we can see it in someone's eyes. Hear it in their voice. It's harder to ignore the quiet cries for help because we've been there, and we remember the times when no one seemed to notice. Or perhaps the times when someone did notice but didn't have time to reach out. Most crushing of all were those times when people reached out, only to judge us or give us trite, simplistic responses.

Compassion walks alongside, trying to understand another's heart. It has empathy and sensitivity. It is willing to embrace those in pain and cry with those who weep.

It is easy to become calloused and to minimize suffering. Our heart can so easily grow hard. Difficulties soften our heart and make us less judgmental. Those who have felt pain see the pain of others. As Jesus saw all the people gather about Him, Scripture tells us that He felt compassion "because their problems were so great and they didn't know what to do or where to go" (Matthew 9:36, TLB).

Compassion has many faces. It is gentle. It is full of mercy and grace. It is love in action. Betsy says she never understood grief until her mother died suddenly in a car accident. Now she knows the emptiness of loss. Kate impatiently told people, "If you can't change it, just get over it!" Then her husband left her and their two young boys for another man. The sting of abandonment and betrayal is something she will never forget.

Hard times changed Betsy and Kate. They reach out more and give less advice. They show love and compassion. I see the gentleness in their eyes and know that if someone was in pain, either one would drop what she was doing and walk the difficult road with the one in need.

Adversity...Strengthens Courage

Laura was shocked when at age thirty-two she was diagnosed with leukemia. She cried and prayed and got angry.

After a two-year battle, now declared symptom free, Laura sat in my office.

"How has this changed you?" I asked.

She smiled. "First of all, I'm thankful for every day. Each moment of life is a wonderful gift. Second, I'm not as fearful. Cancer gives you courage. You know that, *if I can face this, I can face anything.*"

We develop courage by surviving difficult times and challenging adversity. As Mary Tyler Moore put it: "Pain nourishes courage. You can't be brave if you've only had wonderful things happen to you."

Courage is the ability to withstand hardship—the willingness to look fear in the eye and stand firm. Pain and danger mold our courage. Those who have been wounded naturally want to withdraw and retreat. The world no longer seems safe or trustworthy, and even the simplest activities loom before them as feats of courage.

A woman who can face her difficulties without being crushed develops a courage that impacts how she thinks and feels and acts. Life is elastic...it either expands or shrinks based upon how we deal with adversity. It is our courage that shapes our character.

> It is not in the still calm of life, or the repose of a pacific station, that great characters are formed.... Great necessities call out great virtues.
> —Abigail Adams

Adversity...Builds Character

Character is committed to doing what is true, right, good, and wise regardless of the cost. In a season of difficulty and struggle, we find ourselves tempted by the easiest path, rather than the right path. Wounds tempt us to compromise. We justify questionable actions and convince ourselves that they are "acceptable under certain conditions."

Adversity tests who we are—it either strengthens us or weakens us. It shows our character.

A teenage boy responded to a "Help Wanted" sign in a local store window. The owner sent the boy up to the attic—which was dirty, hot, and cramped—to sort several boxes of paperwork. It was a miserable job. At the bottom of the last box, the boy found a ten-dollar bill. With the job finished, he took the money to the owner.

"You passed the test," the owner said. "You completed a hard job without complaint and you showed honesty. It's someone with that sort of character that I want to work for me."

Personally, I have never had a difficulty that didn't make me stronger in some way. And when the pain was at its highest intensity...that was when I grew most.

As I've studied the greatest men and women of human history, it's amazing how many of them experienced severe adversity. In fact, it appears that the very qualities that made them great were forged in the darker days of their lives.

Adversity...Deepens Faith

Hard times and deep wounds remind us of our humanity, our humility, and our utter dependence upon God. Adversity reminds us that we're not nearly as self-sufficient as we'd like to think ourselves. It beckons us to faith. As Pope John Paul II said: "Faith leads us beyond ourselves. It leads us directly to God." I frequently wonder how people can handle difficulties without God. Helen Keller learned through being blind and deaf that "a simple childhood faith...solves all the problems that come to us."

Our wounds drive us closer to God. They force us to our knees as we cry out to Him. Martin Luther wrote that "except under troubles, trials, and vexations, prayer cannot rightly be made."

It's true, isn't it? When everything is sunshine, lollipops, and daisies in our lives, our prayers lose their passion. Ah, but when the darkness falls, when the disappointment comes, when fear descends, that's when we pray with all our heart.

Maybe the old saying is right: "Need teaches us to pray." Desperation improves our perspective and our prayers. Why? Because it leads us back to the arms of God, where we discover all the peace and rest for which we so deeply yearn. As Jesus invites us: "Come to me, all of you who are weary and carry heavy burdens, and I will give you rest" (Matthew 11:28, NLT).

When all is well, we aren't aware of how badly we need God. Yet when difficulties overwhelm us, we know we need Him. George Mueller emphasized this when he wrote: "The only way to learn strong faith is to endure strong trials."

What then, is the greatest enemy to our faith? *It is prosperity.* When everything comes easy for us, we grow lazy, proud, and selfish. When troubles don't push us deeper, our world shrinks to those issues immediately before our nose. Jean de La Bruyere wrote, "Out of difficulties grow miracles."

Without faith, miracles lay unclaimed.

Without difficulty, there appears no need for faith.

In the end, then, it is our wounds that provide wings that catch the currents of faith…and carry us to higher vistas than we would have otherwise known.

God Is Good

Celebrate your wounds, for they make you so much better.
James Emery White says it well:

- If there is any tenderness to my heart, it has come through its being broken.

- If anything of worth flows through my soul, it flows out of a desert.

- If there is any trustworthiness to my mind, it was forged on the anvil of doubt.

- If my actions seem vigorous, they originated in blindness and frailty.

- If there is depth to any of my relationships, it has come through wounding.

183

Let's stop bemoaning our pain and feeling sorry for ourselves. For no matter how difficult our struggles or how deep our wounds, they carry with them great lessons. They teach us much about ourselves, life, and God. They enrich us in ways that nothing else can. They give us the patience to endure, the maturity to grow, the compassion to reach out to others in need, the courage to survive, the character to transform something terribly hurtful into something positive, and the faith to know that we are not alone.

We may indeed go through a season of suffering—in fact, we can count on it. Jesus said, "In this godless world you will continue to experience difficulties. But take heart! I've conquered the world" (John 16:33, *The Message*). For some, that season of hardship and heartache will be longer than for others, but there will come a time when it ends. God promises "he will restore, support, and strengthen you, and he will place you on a firm foundation" (1 Peter 5:10, NLT).

Make no mistake: triumph is best born out of tragedy.

Questions for Reflection

1. How have your wounds influenced your emotional and spiritual growth?

2. How has your hurt made you more compassionate and sensitive? What types of people in pain do you find yourself particularly drawn to?

3. Jean de La Bruyere wrote, "Out of difficulties grow miracles." How have you seen this play out in the lives of others? In what ways have your wounds drawn you closer to God?

4. Identify something positive about your life. Celebrate! Give yourself a gift (a new bottle of nail polish, a magazine or book, a favorite desert, a movie, a new piece of clothing, etc.) to remind yourself that good things are still happening.

Fresh New Beginnings

[Pam]

It is when we are out of options that
we are most ready for God's surprises.

MAX LUCADO

We've all been there. Our jaw drops. Our eyes widen. Our heart pounds. Our boggled mind tries to grasp what we've just heard. In disbelief we wonder, *Is this really happening?*

"I want a divorce."

"The company is downsizing. Your position will no longer be needed."

"This is the school principal. I need to meet with you immediately."

"I never want to hear from you again."

"The cancer is spreading…."

"We're bankrupt."

"I'm sorry. There's nothing more we can do for your loved one…."

"The test results reveal mild traumatic brain injury."

I heard that last one on that gloomy September day after Jessie's accident. In split seconds I was reeling with emotion, wishing I'd soon wake up from a bad dream.

Let's be real. Life is hard. It is a series of challenges, problems, and questions without answers. To think otherwise causes unnecessary anguish. Immense suffering is an integral part of our human condition. We are encouraged to not be surprised by it: "Dear friends, don't be surprised at the fiery trials you are going through, as if something strange were happening to you" (1 Peter 4:12, NLT).

Don't be surprised by suffering. It is part and parcel of living in a fallen world. Instead, be surprised by God's healing power that springs forth from the depths of your pain. God is mighty within you and is committed to restoring you. He is on a mission to revive, refresh, and resurrect the dead places in your soul.

"If you return to me, I will restore you.... I will give you back your health and heal your wounds," says the LORD.

JEREMIAH 15:19; 30:17, NLT

To restore means to bring back to a former or original condition. When we read of God's restoring work in Scripture, we find that He always improves, increases, and multiplies something above and beyond its original condition. When God restored Job after the terrible trials he endured, He gave him twice what he had lost and blessed him more in his latter years of life than when he was in his prime (see Job 42:12–17). Jesus told his followers that if they suffered losses when following Him, He would restore their losses one hundred times over (Mark 10:29–30). God says, "If you return to me, I will restore you" (Jeremiah 15:19, NLT).

It's a beautiful promise. But there's a condition attached, isn't there?

If we return. *If* we do an about-face. *If* we abandon all of our self-redemptive strategies and begin moving towards God, He will restore us.

What does this mean, then? That we make a whole new sheet of resolutions or follow some kind of list full of rules or rituals? No. Our God's deepest desire is a relationship with you and me. It is within a close personal connection with Him that the healing and rebuilding of our lives begins.

Jesus makes a promise to the weak and wounded of this world. He says, "The Spirit of the Sovereign LORD is upon me, because the LORD has appointed me to bring good news to the poor. He has sent me to comfort the brokenhearted and to announce that captives will be released and prisoners will be freed. He has sent me to tell those who mourn that the time of the LORD's favor has come, and with it, the day of God's anger against their enemies. To all who mourn in Israel, he will give beauty for ashes, joy instead of mourning, praise instead of despair" (Isaiah 61:1–3, NLT).

If you were to invite Jesus to visit with you over a cup of tea, He might share His heart using words something like this:

187

I have good news for you. I am with you. I want to comfort you and heal your broken heart. At this very moment, I am pushing back hell and fighting your battles for you. I am avenging you. Before long you will experience the spoils of victory.

I see all the details. You deeply grieve your losses, and your grief is valid. I want to fellowship with you in your suffering. Come to Me. Allow My Spirit to touch your wounds. I promise you: I will replace your devastation and despair with My Spirit of gladness and joy. This isn't something you can do. It is something I will accomplish for you.

188

I have watched God exchange beauty for ashes in the lives of countless women. Just last week, I received a letter from a friend who shared a delightful insight she'd had. It was about God's remarkable ability to touch the wounds we endure, turning them into a launching pad for His plans and purposes.

Dear Pam,

During my elementary years I lived in a variety of cross-cultural situations. Through the fifth grade, I was the only white girl among my Eskimo, African American, and Native American friends.

The year I turned eleven was a time of racial and political unrest. I became increasingly aware that I was different, and hated because I was white. My peers' vicious words and cruel treatment left deep wounds and a permanent scar. Life experience convinced me that girls my age could not be trusted, and that at any moment they would turn on me.

I carried that scar into my college years. But God, in His kindness, was orchestrating events to chip away at the protective wall I had built around my heart. I did some graduate studies at a Bible college, and much of my course work focused on reaching out and helping women. God and I were in a standoff. I kept telling Him, "God, there is no way I'm going to get involved with groups of women. They can't be trusted! Where two or more of them are gathered, evil is in the midst of them."

A few years later God orchestrated another opportunity for my restoration in the school of life. I was a young mother with four boys under the age seven. My husband's business took him out of town weekly, and we lived far from the rest of our family in the Chicago suburbs. The only way I survived those years was because women—groups of women—reached out to me and persistently loved me. During those twelve taxing years, God healed my childhood wound and proved to me that there were women in this world who could be trusted.

Now that my children are older, I'm endeavoring to do for others what was done for me. I lead a ministry in my church, training ladies how to coach and mentor other women. Never, in my wildest imagination, would I have ever thought that I'd discover my greatest joy and passion in deep connections with women. Those I used to run from, I am now compelled to run to. Jesus was right. When two or more are gathered in His name, He IS in the midst of them healing, restoring, and accomplishing the impossible.

Love,

Lynn

New Every Morning

Every morning can be a fresh start—a brand-new opportunity to turn to God. While rolling out of bed we can say a simple prayer. Maybe something like this….

God, I come to You with an open heart. I align myself with You, placing myself under Your authority and tender care. Be my healer. Fill me with Your spirit of joy. Open the eyes of my heart to perceive Your presence with me as we journey through this day together.

This kind of intimate, firsthand contact with God conceives and births times of refreshment. Peter, who endured one wave of affliction after another, talks about the chain of events set in motion when we turn to God: "Now it's time to change your ways! Turn to face God so he can wipe away your sins, [and] pour out showers of blessing to refresh you" (Acts 3:19, *The Message*).

God is the kindest person I have ever met. His attention to detail absolutely wows me beyond words. Time and experience have taught me that He is intimately acquainted with every burden we bear, and that He is absolutely intentional about sending blessings to refresh us when we need them most.

My heart ached the evening I heard the news from the medical neuropsychologist about my daughter Jessie's condition. I knew the road of recovery would be longer and slower than any of us had anticipated. It would require hard work and persistence, with a variety of interventions. Frankly, I was already weary from the past year of plodding through other multiple challenges. This new turn of events left me feeling overwhelmed. I knew I was in over my head…and out of resources.

But God wasn't.

He hadn't even begun to demonstrate His creativity and power. He had some amazing surprises up His sleeve, and a lesson that taught me to leave the business of healing up to Him.

Around nine o'clock that evening, I was brushing my teeth when my husband, John, entered the bedroom waving a check and announced, "We sold the truck!" A buyer had just finalized the deal. He was delighted, and I was halfheartedly enthusiastic. I was still reeling from the news we'd absorbed just a few hours earlier.

As John left the room a quick thought flitted across my mind. *I wonder if we'll be able to get new bedroom furniture soon.* We'd had the same bedroom furniture for twenty-eight years, and I was more than ready to execute an extreme makeover on our bedroom. Over the years I had casually researched bedroom sets and knew precisely what I wanted. The thought left as quickly as it arrived, and we turned out the lights for the night.

The next day I got the kids off to school, met with clients at the counseling center, and returned home around five in the afternoon. I was in the kitchen getting a drink of water when the doorbell rang. The next thing I heard was the pitter-patter of Nathan's feet hitting the tile from his bedroom to the front door. I heard the door open and Nathan say, "NO!" to whoever was standing there.

The walls shook when Nathan slammed the door shut. *That's odd,* I thought, and went to check on Nathan.

"Nathan, who was that?"

"Bad man!" he replied with a scowl.

Now he had my attention. I hurried to the front door, glanced outside, and saw a man walking up the sidewalk to the next house. Curious about who was canvassing our neighborhood, I opened the door and yelled, "Can I help you?"

He turned around, jogged back down the sidewalk, and, with a deep southern drawl, said, "Ma'am, you see that semi up there?" Pointing to a truck up the street, he continued: "That truck is full of furniture from North Carolina. It was supposed to be delivered to a furniture store in Portland, but the store canceled the order. Our company has given us permission to drive the streets of Portland and sell the goods direct off the truck. We've got top-of-the-line couches, recliners, grandfather clocks…you name it, we've got it!"

What kind of a scam is this guy running? I wondered.

Thanking him for the information, I told him I might come out to the truck a bit later. In the meantime I decided to exercise diligence and called the nonemergency police line. After I explained the scenario, the dispatcher on the other end of the line responded, "Yes. We know about this situation. It's kind of strange, but they're legit."

Hmmm. The bargain shopper in me saw flashing blue lights and heard bells and whistles. I walked up the street to take a peek, along with several other neighbors who were already perusing the products. At first glance it was obvious to me that this was high-end merchandise. One of the young men working the truck turned to me and said, "What's your fancy, miss?"

"Do you by any chance have any bedroom sets?" I asked.

"Uh, yes, ma'am, we do. We have one set."

"Is it for a king-sized bed?"

"Yes ma'am, it is."

"Is it, by any chance, cherrywood?"

"Well, as a matter a fact, ma'am, that's exactly what it is. Today must be your lucky day…"

I chuckled at his good-natured salesmanship and asked if I could see the set. Flipping through a stack of brochures, he located a full-color picture and proudly showed it to me.

My mouth dropped open. I could hardly believe what I was seeing. The six-piece set was even more beautiful than what I had been hoping to buy for our bedroom: It had a hand-carved cherrywood four-poster bed; two high-rise nightstands; a roomy armoire; and a full-length dresser with mirror.

Noticing the price at the bottom of the ad, I realized I was out of my league. He must have read my mind, because the next thing out of his mouth was: "Ma'am…do you see that price right there?"

I nodded affirmatively.

"Well, ma'am…today *is* your lucky day…it will be less than a third of that."

The hook was set. He was reeling me in. I promptly ran some simple calculations and concluded…done deal!

"Hold it for me!" I replied. "I need to go get my husband."

John returned to the truck with me and asked the young man if we could please see the furniture.

"Sir…I can only do that if you are really serious about buying this set. It's all wrapped up in cardboard, and we're going to have to unload each piece in your front yard and strip the cardboard off so that you can inspect it. Our company will not pay to ship this furniture back if you decide you don't want it in a few weeks."

John knew the bulldog look in my eyes when he saw it, and assured the man we were very serious. So right there, in front of all the neighbors, this team of young men unloaded all the furniture into our front yard and stripped off the cardboard casings. Each piece was absolutely perfect. We couldn't find a scratch, chip, or ding anywhere. Besides that, the furniture, was far more beautiful than I had ever seen or hoped to buy.

After the inspection was complete, I turned to the young man and said, "We've got one problem. Our bedroom is full of furniture, and I don't have anywhere to put any of this."

In keeping with his gracious southern style, he said, "Oh, ma'am, that's no problem. Just show us where you want the bedroom set to go. We'll haul out the old stuff and move in the new." Four hours later, we handed them a check (with some burgers for the road) and sent them on their way.

At ten o'clock that evening, John and I climbed into our new bed and laughed till our sides ached over this crazy turn of events. The best part about it was that we got brand-new furniture and didn't even have to weather the crowds at the mall!

I laid my head on my pillow, closed my eyes, and breathed a prayer of thanksgiving to God for His generous gifts. Suddenly it occurred to me—just the night before I'd had that flash of an idea about new bedroom furniture. And twenty-four hours later we were lying in it!

God in His kindness was reassuring me:

Pam, if I hear your fleeting thoughts and can deliver furniture to your front door, surely I hear the deeper cries of your heart and can deliver your daughter to the destinations I have planned.

I love it when God uses something concrete to get a message through to me. Our beautiful bedroom set is a tangible and constant reminder that I am to rest in God's ability to do what I cannot do. I must daily turn to Him and put my confidence in the fact that He is good, and everything that matters to us matters to Him.

196

How distressing and discouraging life becomes when we lose sight of God. It's as though we're trying to live on a flat piece of paper, in a two-dimensional world with no depth of meaning or anticipation or joy. We cannot read the Christian life on the basis of individual circumstances. We must not place our focus on individual events such as a heart attack, an illness, or an injury. If we do, we'll lose sight of the fact that there's a wider, deeper picture here. And it's an eternal one. It is a work that God is doing from beginning to end.

—DR. RON MEHL

God is at work in you. He is steadfast in His love and extends an invitation: "Call to me and I will answer you. I'll tell you marvelous and wondrous things that you could never figure out on your own" (Jeremiah 33:3, *The Message*).

If you call, God will answer.

He is for you.

He is your Avenger.

He longs to renew you.

The life-giving waters of His Spirit will bubble up within you, like artesian springs, quenching your thirst and washing away debris that blocks your healing. Day after day, until you take your final breath, He will compassionately attend to your needs. His resources are inexhaustible. His mercies are new every morning (Lamentations 3:22–23, NKJV).

Have you been bulldozed by life? Are you flat on your back with nowhere to look but up? Take your broken heart to Jesus. Invite Him to orchestrate the way through your suffering. Ask Him to blow your mind with His goodness. Tuck in close, and then watch carefully for divine surprises to spring up out of nowhere—both inside and out. Our God specializes in what we think is impossible.

The poet Paul Claudel said it very well: "Jesus did not come to explain away suffering or remove it. He came to fill it with His presence."

Thank You, Lord. Praise Your name. You are the One who restores.

1. God's mercies are new every morning. What challenge are you facing today in which you need God's mercy? Talk openly with Him about these concerns and invite Him to meet your specific needs.

2. As you look back over your life, when have you experienced new beginnings and evidences of God's restoration?

3. Isaiah 61:1–3 is quoted on page 187. As you read this Scripture, what memories or images does it bring to mind about your life? What do you sense God saying to you?

4. God often uses our wounds as a springboard for helping others. Write a letter to someone in pain telling them how God has transformed you through your darker times in life.

Trusting Again

[Steve]

Anything I've ever done that ultimately was
worthwhile...initially scared me to death.

BETTY BENDER

give up! Why would I be stupid enough to ever trust
anybody again?"

Lisa had just discovered that Kyle, her husband of
seven years, had left her and their two children for
another woman—Lisa's best friend. The hurt pierced her
like nothing she had ever felt before. Lisa loved Kyle with
all her heart and thought they'd had a great relationship.
But for the past four years—over half their marriage—Kyle
had been secretly having an affair with Joy. During this
same time, Lisa and Joy met for coffee several times each
week, scrapbooked together, and shared their dreams.

Lisa wanted to die.

Literally. Immediately.

If it hadn't been for her two small children, she might

have ended her life. Sometimes a wound seems so deep that we think we can never recover from it.

In fact, we don't even want to try.

Deep wounds cause us to recoil and retreat. We withdraw and hide away. We promise ourselves that we will never, never let anybody hurt us like that again. We put up strong defenses and build thick walls to guard our heart from the cold winds and harsh cruelties of life. Our goal becomes self-protection, because we honestly wonder if we'd even be able to survive another wound.

Yet the very strategies we employ to avoid harm become traps in themselves—snares with iron jaws that clamp and hold us in our pain. We become so focused on our fear of more pain that we can't heal. We get stuck in a place that seems safe, but blocks us from any real growth.

To trust again is hard.

It involves putting ourselves in a situation where we might be hurt once more. And most of us find this too uncomfortable—or frightening. Our self-protection mechanism may keep us from foolishly offering our trust to someone we know is untrustworthy. Yet to not trust at all because someone *may* be untrustworthy is equally foolish.

To grow we must be intentional. Passivity means remaining stuck in our pain. But to actively step out, regardless of our fears, can open up opportunities that will make us healthier people. The following four choices are crucial to our trusting again.

Choice #1: Accept Reality

Reality isn't always pretty, but it's better than the alternative. Reality is life; it's where we have to live. Acceptance looks unblinkingly at our situation and admits that *this is really how things are at the present moment.*

It may not be how we wish it was.

It may not be what it might have been.

It may not be anything that seems right or logical or fair.

Even so, acceptance says, this is what *is*. This is what I must deal with.

Refusing to either exaggerate or minimize, acceptance simply says, "This is reality…and now, what does God want me to do with it? What is His provision for me at this moment of life?"

Acceptance is the first step to healing. It allows us to evaluate the situation and determine what we might do next. Without acceptance we cannot develop a plan that moves us forward. We get stuck circling the pain and wondering why. As Virginia Satir writes, "Life is not the way it's supposed to be. It's the way it is. The way you cope with it is what makes the difference."

Reality may be harsh. It may throw us punches we never thought we could handle, but with God's help we can deal with more than we ever thought possible. Acceptance is a conscious choice that becomes the foundation on which we build the rest of our lives.

At seventeen Joni broke her neck while diving from a floating dock into Chesapeake Bay. Suddenly, irreversibly, her world changed. Instead of being an active, athletic, independent girl, she was a quadriplegic sentenced to spend the rest of her life in a wheelchair. This was a reality Joni desperately did not want to face, let alone accept. She prayed for healing, for a miracle, for anything to stop this nightmare.

One winter afternoon Joni looked out a window at her parent's home to see her sisters trotting their horses through the snow. Sadness overwhelmed her as she wished she could jump out of her wheelchair and onto a horse to join them. Later that day Joni wheeled her chair outside to listen to the wind whistle through the pines and feel the soft snowflakes melt on her face.

"No, I couldn't ride horseback in the snow," she wrote, "but I could appreciate the pleasure of a snowy evening even while sitting still. Accepting my wheelchair didn't happen right then and there. That snowy evening was just one in a long series of many days when the Holy Spirit covered my hurt with His gentle grace."

As Joni Eareckson Tada accepted her reality, she learned to draw by holding a pencil in her mouth. Soon she became a respected artist. As the years passed she also became a bestselling author and a well-known speaker who has addressed large crowds in thirty-seven countries. Joni is also the founder and president of Joni and Friends, an organization that promotes Christian ministry in the disabled community worldwide. None of this would have happened if Joni had not first accepted her disability.

Acceptance is not sitting back passively to see what happens next. It does not stare at its wound, feeling sorry for itself. It does not get stuck in the illusory worlds of "If-Only" or "What-Might-Have-Been." Acceptance does not give up. It does not cry out to God, "I don't deserve this." Acceptance says, "I don't like this, but I know God can give me the strength to make it through."

Acceptance knows that while wounds may be uncomfortable or difficult to bear for the moment, they may also deliver powerful lessons. Keri West sums it up well when she writes that acceptance "works within today's reality while stretching toward tomorrow's possibility."

And one more thing.

When you think about the reality of what *is,* you must reckon with the ultimate reality of a compassionate, loving, all-powerful God who inhabits this very instant in time. He is the Greater Reality above all other realities. It is in Him that "we live and move and have our being" (Acts 17:28). And though He may not choose to change your circumstances, just as He declined to grant Joni the healing for which she pleaded, He is still God Almighty, *nothing* is too difficult for Him, and you can do all things through Christ who strengthens you (Jeremiah 32:17; Philippians 4:13).

Choice #2: Let Go

Once we accept the reality of our wounds, we must learn to let go. Many of our wounds involve losses—something we had that has been taken away. Maybe we have lost a loved one, a friendship, a cherished hope, a dream. Maybe we've lost our health, our security, our reputation. It's easy to dwell on "the good old days." We all want to hold on to the happier memories of seasons gone by. But this keeps us trapped in the past and (let's face it) a reality that no longer exists.

THINGS TO LET GO OF

unhealthy relationships	negativity
anger	criticism
guilt and shame	self-pity
unrealistic expectations	the need to be right
resentments	pride

Isaiah says to "forget the former things; do not dwell on the past" (Isaiah 43:18). The past is unchangeable. M. Scott Peck writes that contentment is "being at peace with the unchangeable circumstances, choices and mistakes of your past." Letting go moves us forward.

Once we let go of the past, we can let go of the negative emotions associated with the past—the anger, hurt, disappointment, bitterness, sorrow, fear, shame, regret. These negative emotions are a heavy load for anyone to carry. Too heavy. They weigh us down and darken our spirit. The tighter we hold on to them, the more miserable we feel. These feelings become chains that keep us from growth. It's like driving with our eyes so focused on the rearview mirror that we can't see the road in front of us.

Nobody said that letting go was easy!

Jenny's fiancé, Ben, was killed by a drunk driver on the way to their wedding. They had been high school sweethearts and everyone considered them the perfect couple. Suddenly, at twenty-three, he was dead and she was devastated beyond words.

Some twenty years have passed since that dark day, and Jenny is one of the loveliest, brightest, most compassionate people I know. Yet she has never gone out on a date. Oh, she has been asked—hundreds of times. Each time she blushes and politely says that she can't.

Jenny is still in love with Ben.

His picture still occupies a central place on the fireplace mantle of her small house, his letterman's jacket hangs neatly hangs in her closet, and her engagement ring remains suspended from a gold chain around her neck. Until Jenny can let go of Ben, she will never be happy.

Choice #3: Risk

Life is a risk. Anything really worthwhile requires a risk. We risk being hurt again, we risk embarrassment, we risk losing what we have. Risks are as much a part of living as oxygen is part of the atmosphere. Every day delivers a fresh supply of risks to our doorstep.

In the wake of being wounded, however, we seek to

avoid risks. We want to wrap up in a cozy quilt and snuggle into an overstuffed chair with a glowing fire at our feet.

We don't want to face the storms of life.

We don't want to deal with any more pressure or trauma.

We don't want to be afraid again or grieved again or disappointed again.

So we pull the blinds and cuddle up in that big soft quilt and refuse to go anywhere or do anything or expose ourselves in any way.

We might call this kind of existence "safety and security."

In fact, it's a living death.

Without risk we can neither grow nor improve. We grow stale and stagnant. To avoid risk puts us in danger of living a life regretting what might have been. As Geena Davis says, "If you risk nothing then you risk everything."

Risk takes courage. It takes stepping out into the scary unknown. Risk involves facing our fears and counting on the fact that a loving God remains in control of the details of our lives. David prayed, "I trust in you, O LORD; I say, 'You are my God.' My times are in your hands." The apostle Paul wrote, "If God is for us, who can ever be against us?" (Psalm 31:14–15; Romans 8:31, NLT).

There is no real risk with God at our side. Moses gave instructions to the people of Israel that before any battle the priests were to stand before the warriors and say, "Do not be afraid as you go out to fight today! Do not lose heart or panic. For the LORD your God is going with you!" (Deuteronomy 20:3–4, NLT).

Years ago I heard a saying that I repeat to myself whenever fear gets a hold on me: "Fear paralyzes faith, but faith paralyzes fear." If we keep our eyes focused on the object of our fear, our fear will grow. But if we focus on the object of faith, our faith grows. The apostle Peter discovered the truth of this as Jesus called him to walk across the churning surface of the sea one wild, black night. As long as Peter kept his eyes on Jesus, he could do the impossible. But as soon as he looked at the waves, he sank.

Fear tells us that we can't do it. Faith tells us that with God all things are possible. Philip Yancey writes that faith "involves learning to trust that, out beyond the perimeter of fog, God still reigns and has not abandoned us, no matter how it may appear."

Risk means reaching out in spite of our fears. Florence Nightingale wrote: "How very little can be done under the spirit of fear." Yet with faith amazing things can happen. With faith we have the courage to risk…and those risks bring with them tremendous rewards. I agree with Leo Buscaglia: "The person who risks nothing…may avoid suffering and sorrow, but he simply cannot learn and feel and change and grow and love and live."

Risking is crucial to moving beyond your wounds and using your pain as a springboard to a deeper faith. Trusting that God has our best interest in mind, risk holds on to faith and lets loose of fear. It's knowing that whatever happens, He will be our rock and refuge. Jeremiah said it well when he wrote: "But blessed are those who trust in the LORD and have made the LORD their hope and confidence. They are like trees planted along a riverbank, with roots that reach deep into the water. Such trees are not bothered by the heat or worried by long months of drought" (Jeremiah 17:7–8, NLT).

Choice #4: Patience and Persistence

Healing rarely comes quickly. It frequently moves slowly, one baby step at a time. Sometimes our growth is barely perceptible. Sometimes it takes three steps forward and two steps back. Sometimes we feel stuck in neutral, wondering if anything will ever change.

The twenty-first century is an impatient world. We want things *now*. Instantaneously. Do you recall the personal computers of ten or fifteen years ago? We thought they were wonderful. The cutting edge. Did it ever occur to us that booting up a program or saving a document "took too long"? Are you kidding? It was only a matter of seconds. But if we went back to those machines now, the pauses and delays would drive us crazy. We're used to instant everything.

And when things don't happen as quickly as we think they should, we get angry...or simply give up. In his powerful classic, *The Imitation of Christ*, Thomas à Kempis writes: "All men commend patience although few are willing to practice it."

Maybe so...yet to grow and heal, we all need to learn patience. For no matter how hard we work, God is ultimately in control of when things happen. As Peter Marshall prayed: "Teach us, O Lord, the disciplines of patience, for to wait is often harder than to work."

Patience is an act of faith. Once we risk, we must wait. David tells us to "be still in the presence of the LORD, and wait patiently for him to act…. Travel steadily along his path" (Psalm 37:7, 34, NLT). Impatience takes us nowhere positive; in fact, it frequently increases our frustration and irritability—adding to our anger, fear, shame, and sorrow. Patience steps forward, trusting God to get us where He wants us when He sees fit.

Patience never comes into our lives empty-handed…it always brings an armload of incomparable rewards, including wisdom, faith, and peace.

Patience has a sister. Did you know that? Her name is *Persistence*. Persistence simply refuses to give up. While Patience waits, Persistence waits and waits and *waits*. Great things take time to accomplish. Houses take time to build, books take time to write, seeds take time to grow and bloom into beautiful flowers. Calvin Coolidge said: "Nothing in the world can take the place of persistence." The determination to keep running the race when your sides ache and your legs are worn out is self-discipline in action. Persistence falls down five times, but stands up six.

Catherine Marshall struggled with terrible fears, but she would not let them control her. After she married Peter, they moved to Washington, DC, where he became pastor of a prestigious church and chaplain of the U.S. Senate. A few years later she was diagnosed with tuberculosis. Catherine spent the next two years isolated in her room, struggling with this disease. The pain was great, and the loneliness and depression were worse. With persistence Catherine pushed forward until her health returned and her depression subsided.

Then, without warning, Peter died suddenly of a heart attack. Catherine's world collapsed, and this time she wondered whether she'd ever make it through. But her persistence forced her to accept reality, let go of her fear, and risk. Soon Catherine was a bestselling author and a world-renowned speaker. Later she wrote: "The strengthening of faith comes through staying with it in the hour of trial."

210

Anything Is Possible

Once we've been wounded, we want to do whatever we can to keep from being wounded again. We grow wary and careful. Sometimes our worries keep us up all night, and sometimes our fears paralyze us during the day. We might avoid certain people or places or activities. Our wounds steal our innocence, and we often feel like we'll never trust as completely as before. If we aren't careful, our wounds shrink our world and its amazing possibilities.

The only way to grow is by learning to trust again.

I love it when Moses said, "Oh, that you would choose life" (Deuteronomy 30:19, NLT). That is our wish for you.

Remember Lisa? Remember how she wanted to die

when Kyle left her for Joy? During the next year she experienced every negative emotion possible—from anger and hatred to sorrow and shame. She spent many hours crying and feeling sorry for herself.

Then one morning she looked in the mirror and realized how pathetic she looked. She decided at that moment that she could either let her wound destroy her...or she could live life again.

So she brushed her hair, put on her makeup, and drove to the mall to buy a new outfit. Then she called some friends and met them for lunch. Over the next week she accepted her situation, let go of her anger and hurt, and started taking risks again. On that day, she chose to live and trust again.

Did her choice make the next day easier?

No; all of the pain and difficulties and sorrows came rushing back as she sat on the edge of her bed and rubbed the sleep from her eyes.

Yet Lisa chose to move ahead, one day at a time. As the months passed, it *did* get easier. Yes, there were relapses. But for every relapse, Lisa would intentionally take another risk.

When Lisa met Chad she was terrified. What if he was a jerk? What if he hurt her? What if he was untrustworthy? They dated for two years, fell in love, and are now married. Chad has adopted Lisa's two children, and this new family is happier than Lisa ever thought possible. If we asked Lisa today whether it was worth trusting again, she would smile and say, "If I hadn't risked trusting again, I would never have discovered how good God can be."

1. What pain from the past is bogging you down? What is blocking you from letting go? Is it confusing thoughts? Overwhelming feelings? Indecision?

2. What fears keep you from taking the necessary risks to move forward? What is one specific risk you can take today to begin moving forward?

3. Healing requires patience. What do you tell yourself that keeps you from being able to relax when things don't go according to your timetable?

4. Deuteronomy 30:19 reveals God's heart for each one of us. *"Oh, that you would choose life"* (NLT). What does this mean to you? What can you do today that symbolizes you are choosing life?

Please Be Kind to You

[Pam]

> Renewal and restoration are not luxuries.
> They are essentials....There is absolutely nothing enviable
> or spiritual about...a nervous breakdown, nor is an
> ultra-busy schedule...the mark of a productive life.
>
> CHUCK SWINDOLL

a friend of mine recently had her gallbladder removed. As an executive assistant, she was used to having a lot of energy and maintaining a high level of productivity.

But recuperation was taking its toll.

When she complained to her doctor that she still felt tired six weeks after the surgery, her doctor said, "Following this type of surgery, the body heals at a rate of 15 percent per month from the inside out—*if* a person rests and takes good care of himself. If you push too hard, you'll delay your recovery."

When life delivers a hard blow leaving us with a painful emotional wound, it's as if our psyche goes through major surgery. We must be kind to ourselves and give ourselves *time and rest* to recover. But for many of us immersed in this high-speed, sound bite, technological culture, it seems as if "rest" is a four letter word. We push, push, push, to do, do, do, and neglect our basic needs. Unfortunately, life lived in five-speed overdrive either arrests or delays the healing process.

When I was in my early thirties, one of my mentors said to me, "Pam, you are the only one who can take care of you. Don't limit yourself to leftover scraps of energy. You're in a marathon, not a sprint. You must pace yourself."

At that particular time, I was in graduate school, assisting my husband John in working with over three hundred youth, and writing my first book, *Empty Arms,* after the loss of our first baby.

My mentor noticed my fatigue.

In an effort to help me restore balance, she encouraged me to be kind to myself by embracing the bare basics: sleep, reduced stimulation, and realistic expectations. She knew that if I subtracted one or more of these components from the equation, I ran the risk of burning out and not being the person I really wanted to be.

The Power of Sound Sleep

Years ago, I attended a professional seminar with a Harvard-trained psychologist who specialized in treating people suffering from anxiety and depression. He made a statement that left a lasting impression on me: "Many patients can reduce their anxiety and depression symptoms by half if they'll sleep eight to nine hours a night."

That made sense to me. Because of the intricate way our Creator put us together, it's really impossible to attain sound mental health if we deprive our bodies and ignore our basic physical needs.

Lack of rest, of course, is a common American dilemma. We work, raise families, build marriages, tend friendships, and try to wedge in recreational activities. Our daily planners are chock-full of to-do lists, and there are never enough hours in a day to get "it" all done.

True as this may be, we need to remember that sleep is one of the primary ways the body renews itself. It's common knowledge that people who try to live on less than four or five hours of sleep for an ongoing period of time are at higher risk for early death. On the other hand, medical experts agree that consistent, sound sleep reduces emotional turmoil and empowers us to manage life stress.

215

Those who have suffered trauma frequently struggle with insomnia, the inability to fall asleep or stay asleep.

PHYSICAL CAUSES OF INSOMNIA

- *arthritis or other types of chronic pain*
- *endocrine disturbances*
- *overuse of certain chemical substances such as caffeine and decongestants*
- *withdrawal from alcohol or pain medication*
- *disturbances in our biological clock resulting from travel across time zones or from feeding newborn babies during the wee hours of the morning*

But emotional conflicts related to grief, depression, anxiety, and chronic stress can also cause difficulties with sleep. When this is the case, a vicious cycle can set in. High stress causes insomnia, and insomnia causes increased stress. The cycle has to be broken for the brain chemistry to restore itself.

None of our babies slept through the night at an early age, so in the months after they were born, my routine included many midnight feedings. The babies' needs and my shifting hormones meant months of interrupted sleep. When my body didn't renew itself well during the night, my motivation and energy levels were low the following day. I found myself more easily agitated, anxious, and overalert. There were times when I startled awake in the middle of the night even though everyone else in the house was sound asleep and there were no external noises. It was as if my body was sending signals that put me into a 911 mode when there were no logical reasons for alarm.

For my own sanity, I knew I needed to do something to stop the sleep deprivation, but I felt stuck. The babies needed to eat, and I was their source. John and I considered a number of options and then formed a plan. He offered to supplement my nursing by giving the babies one bottle feeding a night so I could get four to five hours of solid sleep. To recharge my batteries for the rest of the day, I also made a point of napping for at least thirty minutes during the day while the little ones slept. The household chores had to take a backseat to my health.

After we established this new routine, I noticed a marked difference. My overall mood improved, and I had more energy during the day. Decision making became easier, chores didn't seem as taxing, and little annoyances didn't escalate into major issues. A few weeks later, the random startle responses I'd been experiencing in the middle of the night subsided.

I recently learned that 40 percent of women over the age of forty experience periodic insomnia. Research scientists speculate that this correlates with the shifting hormone levels that occur prior to menopause. Incidentally, women are more likely to suffer from insomnia than men. Dieting, which women tend to do more often than men, can lower body temperature and interfere with sound sleep.

When we are enduring stressful hardships, our bodies may need even more sleep than usual. I remember talking with a mother whose eleven-month-old son had died after complications from a surgery. "All I want to do is sleep," she said.

One of the red flags of depression is the desire to sleep more than necessary, but I sensed that something else was going on. After her baby died, this woman had begun a new, full-time job and was averaging ten-hour days as an executive assistant. When I asked her how much she slept, she said, "From nine at night to seven in the morning," as if this were a ridiculous amount of time to be in bed. It never crossed her mind that her body needed more sleep because of the heavy emotional burden she was bearing, having recently lost her son and started a new job.

From my perspective, those ten hours of sleep didn't point to pathology…they indicated good self-care.

All of us have probably found ourselves in problem situations that don't faze us when we're well rested, but threaten to level us when we are sleep deprived. The body needs time to renew, reenergize, and replenish itself when we are carrying heavy emotional loads.

If you find yourself irritable, agitated, anxious, or unable to turn off the lights in your brain at night, physical exercise is required, not optional. Although I'm not an expert in physiology, as a clinical counselor I know the mental and emotional benefits of exercise. Studies have shown that it is a cheap, easy way to elevate mood, decrease agitation, and deliver a sense of calm to the brain. The endorphins released during aerobic exercise are powerful mood elevators and natural tranquilizers.

Exercising for the sake of enhancing our emotional state only requires thirty to forty minutes several times a week. We don't have to spend long hours in the gym. Some experts say that maintaining a consistent training-level heart rate for twenty-five minutes will alter the brain chemistry in the same way an antidepressant does. Since it takes a few minutes to work the heart up to a training-level pulse, I encourage my clients to set aside a minimum of thirty minutes for aerobic activity.

Your body will never lie to you. If you feel restless, on edge, and unable to sleep at night, pay attention to your physical needs. To improve your sleep, you might want to consider some of the following suggestions:

- Don't drink caffeine or eat foods with caffeine (chocolate) within six hours of bedtime.

- Don't use decongestants within six hours of bedtime. A twenty-four-hour, time-release decongestant can interrupt your sleep. Antihistamines are a good alternative at night because they tend to cause drowsiness.

- Don't drink alcohol within four to six hours of bedtime. Although it may initially make you drowsy, it can disrupt sound sleep.

- Don't exercise within four hours of bedtime. The hormones released in the brain during exercise can interrupt sleep. Optimum sleep seems to occur when exercise is done approximately six hours before going to bed.

- Take a hot bath or try some other relaxing activity during the hour before bedtime to allow the body to calm down naturally.

- Sip a soothing herbal tea while reading a good book in a quiet, comfortable place.

If you try doing these things yet *still* find yourself unable to sleep, well, it's probably time to consult with your doctor. Some physicians suggest trying an antihistamine at bedtime to help induce sleep. Other sleep aids can be used short term to break a pattern of insomnia and get you back on track.

You might also want to talk with a trained nutritionist about using vitamin and mineral supplements. A number of items such as valerian root, kava kava, melatonin, and chamomile are known to calm the central nervous system. Small adjustments can make a big difference. Even if you increase your sleep by only thirty minutes a night, your brain will reward you with improved functioning.

Reduce Stimulation

For a few months following the death of our first baby, I was emotionally ravaged by grief and worried that we would never be able to have children. The stress of the loss and the hormonal changes in my body left me feeling very fragile. Prior to the loss of our baby, my husband and I had routinely read the newspaper in the morning before work and watched the news at the end of the day.

After we lost our baby, however, I couldn't watch movies, listen to songs, or sit through television programs heavily laden with intense emotional content. The excessive stimulation tied up my stomach in knots. I simply did not have the emotional stamina to metabolize that much bad news all at once.

Grief has a way of distorting our perception. Everything already seems bad, and piling more bad on top of what already seems bad just makes us feel worse.

For several months I had to carefully screen what I listened to, read, and viewed. I skipped the newspaper and chose more uplifting reading material that bolstered my spirit. The Scriptures and devotional books calmed my nerves and brought comfort. Though I didn't like the idea of being less in touch with what was going on in the world, I did enjoy more peace of mind.

Instrumental music with soothing harmonies also had a calming effect on my emotions. Positive input from the outside helped to quiet my inner turmoil and fortified me to do the grief work I needed to do.

As I've worked with people in my counseling office during the last twenty-five years, I've noticed a new trend that has the potential of complicating emotional healing. More and more I'm meeting clients who spend long hours in the evening after work, or after the kids are in bed, on the Internet.

For those who are somewhat socially anxious, being online can seem to be a safer place to interact with others. There is no face-to-face contact, and if they don't want to continue interacting with someone, they can click off-line with one push of a button.

Please don't get me wrong. I use the Internet regularly for a variety of purposes. It's a wonderful tool. But problems arise when the Net becomes a main source of relationships or when the stimulating impact of the activity robs you of sleep or interaction with family members and friends.

Virtual friendships cannot meet our needs for healthy human connection because much of what is perceived online is only a small portion of reality—the reality the other person wants you to see in the written word—not the complete picture of who he or she actually *is*.

I've met men and women who were duped into thinking they had met Prince Charming or Miss Perfect in chat rooms online. It was a heartbreaking and rude awakening when they eventually found out that they had wasted hours, even months, of their lives on some fanciful illusion presented in text. Worse yet, I've talked with clients who unwittingly interacted with smooth-talking users and abusers. What started as an innocent conversation in a chat room led to a scary and troublesome series of events. I don't want to be a gloom-and-doomer, but I do want to suggest exercising healthy caution and setting time limits for online interactions.

Research supports the importance of keeping things in balance. I recently read a study funded by a group of computer companies. Researchers went to a town in Pennsylvania and selected homes that did not have Internet access. The families who agreed to participate in the study were given a computer and Internet access in exchange for the researchers' right to study them for two years.

At the beginning and end of the test period, the participants took a psychological test. I don't think the computer companies expected the results they received. At the end of two years, the study revealed that those individuals who spent more than one hour online per day were significantly more depressed than before they had access to the Internet.[3]

We don't have to take an all-or-nothing approach.

Balance is the key. When we're trying to recover from an emotional wound, we need to take inventory of what is assaulting our senses. Sometimes the media and computers are diversions to escape our pain. But if we are being bombarded with toxic and emotionally intense messages, or if the time we spend in these activities is robbing us of needed rest or time with loved ones, we might actually be complicating or prolonging our healing.

A wise old sage by the name of Peter once wrote, "Whoever would love life and see good days...must seek peace and pursue it" (1 Peter 3:10–11). Are you up for a challenge? Even small adjustments that reduce stimulation can have a positive emotional impact. Why not be kind to yourself? Quiet some of that outside noise for a week or two, and see if your world seems like a more peaceful place to live.

223

Revise Expectations

They say you get what you expect. But then, what do "they" know anyway?

Launi expected to be married happily ever after. It didn't happen.

Tammy, Jackie, Martin, and Len expected their partners to be faithful. They weren't.

Bob and Dave expected their company revenues to increase 25 percent last year. Instead, they both filed for bankruptcy.

Karen and Phil expected their son to go to college in

the fall. He died in a motorcycle accident this spring.

Darcey, Mira, Judy, and I expected to give birth to healthy babies. Yet each of us has a child with special needs.

Recently I came across a Scripture that spoke to me about suffering and expectations: "Then [Jesus] told them what they could *expect* for themselves: 'Anyone who intends to come with me has to let me lead. You're not in the driver's seat—I am. Don't run from suffering; embrace it. Follow me and I'll show you how. Self-help is no help at all'" (Luke 9:23–24, *The Message*, emphasis mine).

As card-carrying members of the human race, we are to expect suffering. Expect heartache. Expect pain and disappointment. Expect the unexpected. Yet while all this is true, we can also expect that as we give God the lead, He will give us what we need to endure the wounds we experience. He will show us how to navigate the raging storms that sweep over the horizon of our lives.

When we are trying to heal from life's painful blows, we need to be especially kind to ourselves by revising our expectations to better fit the reality of our current situation.

As Dr. Stephens stated in a previous chapter, we must accept the truth: What is, is. To continue to hang on to expectations unsupported by facts will simply drive us deeper into a black hole of despair. If we want to heal and improve the quality of our life, we have to let go of unrealistic expectations.

Ever since our youngest was born with Down syndrome, I have had to periodically take inventory of my expectations and make some adjustments.

I can't expect Nathan to read a book out loud or write a book report as our other children did when they were in grade school. If I hang on to that expectation, I will perpetuate my pain and frustrate Nathan. But *I can expect* him to read. That is a tangible, reachable goal for him.

I can't expect that John and I will be empty nesters in a few years, as we had previously thought. But *I can expect* that whatever comes will in some way be good, and that God will be with us.

I can't expect God to shield my children from all adversity and heartache. I can't expect their lives to be pain free. The absence of pain doesn't exist this side of heaven. But *I can expect* God's grace and kindness to be sufficient for their every situation. I can expect God to transform any harsh reality that assaults them into something that ultimately works for their highest good and His greatest glory.

I can't expect myself to always be a wise, patient, and attentive woman. I want to be, of course, but many times I fall short. When I'm tired, I snap at my kids. When I find twenty-five messages waiting for me on my voice mail, I want to run away from everything. Although I try very hard, I'm not always who or what I want to be. But *I can expect* God to pour grace over my weaknesses as I offer them to Him, and to provide strength and time to restore.

In times of weakness I realize once again how profound and desperate is my need for God and His power to change me. That's when I have to hold tightly to the expectation that He will finish the work He has started in me. That's when I must stand on the promise that His power in me "is able to [carry out His purpose and] do superabundantly, far over *and* above all that we [dare] ask or think [infinitely beyond our highest prayers, desires, thoughts, hopes, or dreams]" (Ephesians 3:20, AMP).

Life doesn't always dish out what we expect. But if we remain open to new possibilities, the road ahead can be an adventure. The scenery may not be what we would have chosen or anything like what we imagined, but it can be very, very good indeed. One way or another, God will get us to our final destination in heaven. And then, the fullness of His kindness will be unveiled, and *every expectation we've ever had will fall absurdly short of reality.*

Until that day arrives, please, be kind to you.

Lean in and Relax

It's amazing what kids can teach us about life. I want to share an experience I had with my son, Nathan, when I was deeply mourning the losses he suffers because of Down syndrome. This was another one of those occasions when the Lord spoke to me with a picture.

One afternoon as I watched Nathan in physical therapy, God taught me a lesson about resting in Him.

Shortly after Nathan was born, we enrolled him in an early intervention program in which therapists exercised his mind and body to enhance his development. As an infant,

Nathan's interventions were one-on-one; but as a toddler, he was moved into a classroom setting with several special-needs children.

During the first part of class, the children met in a large, open room where a physical therapist led them in exercises designed to strengthen muscle tone and develop motor skills. Upbeat music filled the room while the children made their best efforts to accomplish simple toe touches, arm reaches, handclaps, bends, and stretches.

I recalled watching similar routines when my two children Jessie and Ben were in preschool. "Head and shoulders, knees and toes," the kids had chimed along with the tape, keeping their motions in cadence with the music. Their movements jibed with the beat. Their actions were precise, clearly defined, and consistent.

But Nathan's class was a much different picture.

The children's motions were awkward and rarely in sync with the leader's. If one of the children happened to dance in rhythm, it was more often than not a happy accident.

But a day came when Nathan lit up with a sense of pride while delivering a perfect performance. He was in step with the therapist through the entire song. He didn't miss a beat. All his gestures were right on the mark. It wasn't because John and I had practiced with him umpteen times at home, and it wasn't because his muscle tone had miraculously changed from floppy to firm.

On that particular day, Nathan had been selected for a demonstration. The therapist asked him to come to the front of the room and stand facing the class while she stood behind him.

"Nathan, lean back into me and put your hands in my hands," she instructed.

I watched Nathan relax his body into hers and place his little hands in her palms. When the music began, the therapist guided Nathan's arms through the routine. *One, two, three, four. Up, down, all around. Together. Apart. Clap, clap, clap.*

Nathan's droopy little arms did everything they were supposed to do as he let go and yielded to her lead. His assignment was to lean in and relax. The rest of the work was up to the therapist. Nathan's weakness was his greatest strength that day.

I embarrassed myself during that class. There we were in the middle of "up, down, clap, clap, clap," and I was wiping tears from my eyes. I secretly wondered if the other parents were thinking, *What's the big deal? She sure gets worked up over her son being picked to lead exercises!*

But there was more to it than that.

The Lord was speaking to me, speaking clearly and tenderly through my son. He showed me my need to lean back and rest in the safety of my Father's arms. He nudged me to let go of the things that were troubling me.

With a keen awareness of my own handicaps, I sensed the Lord reassuring me that His grace is sufficient for me. Should I lose my balance and stumble over bumps on my journey, God will steady me and hold me up. When I get out of step, He will help get me back in sync. The greater my weakness, the greater God's strength displayed in me.

I don't have to be strong to be strong. Nor do you.

As we learn to rest in God, time becomes our friend. As it passes, we begin to experience spiritual and emotional healing. One day we realize we don't feel quite as much pain today as we did last week or last month. We laugh a little more, and the black cloud that comes and goes doesn't hang around as long. We remember, but the pain diminishes. We begin to realize the days of mourning are giving way to newfound joys.

We sense the strong arms of our Redeemer carrying us through the valley of dark shadows. We trust that He is moving us forward in His plans and purposes, ushering us into the bright, wide-open spaces of His grace. All in good time, we come to know Him as the One who transforms our "Valley of Troubles into a Door of Hope," and eventually we will find ourselves, "singing with joy as in days long ago" (Hosea 2:15, TLB).

1. When was the last time you had a great night's sleep? What is most apt to keep you from sound sleep?

2. What activities calm and relax you the most? How often are you involved in these activities? Please double your efforts here.

3. What are three unrealistic expectations you have about things in your life? How do these set you up for disappointment?

4. Find a good book, a magazine, or a favorite movie. Sit in a comfortable chair with your favorite beverage and simply enjoy!

Tell Your Story

[Steve]

God has given you a wonderful story.
Don't waste it.

UNKNOWN

Kim loved both her parents.

At nine years old, a divorce was tearing her apart. Her heart was broken and the pain was beyond words. She watched her father fall into a depression that only grew darker and darker. When it seemed as if life could get no worse, her father killed her mother and then took his own life.

Kim's grief was more than she could handle; for days on end she could not stop crying. She moved in with her grandparents, who bought her a small horse to distract her from her wounds. Riding Firefly became Kim's refuge from a shattered life. Racing across the landscape, she rode so fast that her tears were blown from her eyes and her troubles were left behind. Over time Kim's wounds healed, and she married a wonderful man.

Then God gave Kim a dream.

He let her know that her story need not be wasted. She realized that just as a horse saved her life and healed her wounds, it could be true for other children. So from her story came Crystal Peaks Youth Ranch, a nonprofit ranch that pairs neglected horses with children in pain to create a place of healing and hope.

A dark night can give way to a glorious sunrise. And a tragic wound can set the stage for a wonderful story. In a book entitled *Hope Rising*, Kim Meeder tells her story and the stories of children at her camp. On the last page of the book, she writes: "Like standing on a mountainous trail, we can *choose* which way to go…. When confronted by pain, we can *choose* to take the descending trail that most often leads to a dark and lonely place…. Or we can select the ascending trail and, with some effort and perseverance, we can *choose* to allow our pain to motivate us toward becoming better people, to move us toward a better place."

That ascending trail involves transforming our pain into a promise of hope. The best way to do this is by telling our story.

Speaking Out

Stories should not be hidden away. Our story is very important—a significant part of who we are. It can teach, encourage, and inspire others. It can change their lives.

When Jesus says, "Don't hide your light under a basket! Instead, put it on a stand and let it shine for all" (Matthew

5:15, NLT), He is talking about our lives—our whole lives. Throughout the Old Testament, we are told to remember what God has done. Asaph, one of the writers of the Psalms, declared:

> I recall all you have done, O LORD;
>> I remember your wonderful deeds of long ago.
> They are constantly in my thoughts.
>> I cannot stop thinking about them.
> (Psalm 77:11–12, NLT)

Not only were they in this good man's thoughts, but he wrote them down so he could tell others. And here we are some four thousand years later responding to those very words!

We all need to be prepared to tell our story at any time and in any place. It's amazing how sharing our hurts breaks down walls between people. It connects us with others and opens hearts. Suddenly, pride and pretense disappear. We are now two wounded travelers seeking God's grace and comfort.

It takes *courage* to tell our story, for we must expose our wounds and make ourselves vulnerable. It also takes *compassion*, for as our hearts break over the hurts of others, we yearn to do something to ease their pain. Our story links us to their story and their pain. And as we stand beside them showing our wounds, they no longer feel as isolated or alone.

Speaking out requires preparation. We need to think through what we want to say. As we speak, we need to be able to answer the following questions:

- What is my wound?

- When did it happen?

- What did I feel?

- How did I respond?

- What did God do?

- What did I learn?

- How can I continue to use my wounds to help others?

Organizing our thoughts helps us to speak more clearly. Please be honest. Don't make your descriptions of what happened better or worse than the way things were. Realize that an honest story is frequently more powerful than a perfectly told story.

As a psychologist, I listen to people's stories all day long. I love my job, and I love hearing these stories. They touch my heart and stretch my faith. I wish everybody could hear the stories of searching and struggle that I have heard.

HOW TO SHARE YOUR STORY

1. Relax

2. Keep it simple

3. Keep it short

4. Be real

5. Answer their questions

6. Share what you have learned

7. Show hope

8. Encourage at every opportunity

Stories change lives…but only if they are told.

The oldest of three sisters, Lori grew up in a strong Christian home. But at twenty-one, she found herself single and pregnant. Afraid to tell anyone, she went alone one cold December morning to a clinic and had an abortion.

A year later Lori came to my office, filled with guilt and shame, to tell her story. We spoke of forgiveness and freedom, but Lori was too frightened to share her story with anyone else.

Two years passed, and Lana came to my office. She was the middle child of three sisters. She grew up in a strong Christian family, but at twenty found herself single and pregnant. Afraid to tell anyone, she went alone one April morning to a clinic and had an abortion. We spoke of forgiveness and healing, but Lana was too afraid to share her story with anyone, especially her family.

Another two years passed, and Lucy came to my office. She was the baby of three sisters. At twenty-one she found herself single and pregnant. Not knowing anyone who would understand, she went alone to a clinic and had an abortion. We spoke of forgiveness, and I encouraged her to talk to her older sisters.

She told me that Lori and Lana would never understand. They were perfect sisters and would reject her for bringing disgrace on the family.

My heart broke. Three wounded sisters, each afraid to tell her story—when they could have encouraged and comforted and helped each other so much. As far as I know, not one of these three has yet had the courage to share her story with the others. How terribly sad!

The Seven S's

Telling our story takes determination, humility—and the enthusiastic embracing of each of the following steps:

We Need to Stop

It's easy to keep quiet and bury our pain deep in our heart. Fear of rejection or embarrassment may reinforce our silence. But years of working with men and women in crisis have convinced me that wounds carefully hidden away end up hurting more.

For one thing, how can anyone offer you any comfort if you've hidden your pain from others? In fact, our silence is often selfish, for we can easily become more concerned with protecting ourselves than helping others. We each have a powerful story of how we have dealt with difficult situations. We have learned lessons, developed insights, and gained perspective. To keep quiet about these is to waste your pain. We need to stop being silent.

We Need to Stand Up

We need to admit our wounds. Since we all have our hurts and hurdles, we need to stop pretending all is well and stand up to the truth. Fifteen-year-old Tia wrote her story of rejection and abandonment on the Internet. She closed with: "It was really hard for me to share my story, but I wanted to help someone else out there."

It takes courage to stand up and speak out, but one person who shares encourages others to do the same. Soon we are not alone, and the negative cycle of hopelessness, helplessness, and despair can be broken.

We Need to Search

We are surrounded by people who may be struggling. Yet we are so busy, distracted, or self-absorbed that we don't notice those right in front of us who are in pain. Sometimes, perhaps, we do notice…but since we don't know what to do or say, we ignore them.

Most people dealing with pain leave little clues—for anyone who might be caring enough to notice. Some of the clues are intentional: sad little comments, sighs, frowns, tears, or maybe just staring out a window. Other clues are unintentional—but every bit as clear: the dark circles under the eyes, the distractedness, the sagging shoulders.

We need to search, looking and listening, for those who yearn for our encouragement. Then we can reach out and let them know they are not alone. People need to know they are valued and appreciated, especially when they find themselves trapped in the vortex of their suffering.

We Need to Speak

Some people open their hearts easily; others struggle to find the right words. Part of what adds meaning and purpose to our own wounds is to be able to communicate to others at least some of what we have endured.

Katherine, a twenty-year-old single mother, wrote, "My prayers are with other victims, especially those who have been brave enough to share their personal stories which have been an inspiration to me."

Our words, whether written, spoken, or sung, can give hope and encouragement to anyone who hears them, but especially to those still struggling.

We Need to Serve

Volunteering to help those in difficult situations provides a nonverbal means of providing support and care. Service is love in action, and it allows us to give, just as others gave to us in our time of desperation. (It may also open up opportunities for us to tell our story.) To help others in whatever way we can is an affirmation that our wounds did not minimize or destroy us. Instead, they made us and defined us. Our wounds shape us into better servants.

We Need to Smile

Who can overestimate the power of a smile and a positive attitude to infuse a struggling soul with hope? When others hear our story and see that we can be upbeat and hopeful in spite of the pain, they have something to hold on to. What a powerful influence for good!

Think of what it's like on a dreary, overcast afternoon when the clouds part for an instant and a shaft of sunlight illumines a forest path or turns a rain-wet street into molten gold.

That's what a genuine, warm greeting, a light heart, and a positive attitude can become for someone in the grip of discouragement. We become an example that there is light beyond the darkness. Wounded people feel like their pain will never end—like their landscape will be desolate forever.

But a simple smile and a heart strengthened with hope in God tell them to keep on fighting.

Allison, currently a thirty-five–year-old corporate executive whose arms were badly burned and scarred, told me her story of depression and self-hatred. Then she smiled and said, "Use me in your book! Tell them if I can make it, anybody can. Just don't give up."

We Need to Show

We need to show the world that most of our limits are in our mind. With God's help we do things we thought would be impossible.

Remember the exultant prayer of David?

For by You I can run upon a troop;
  And by my God I can leap over a wall.
(Psalm 18:29, NASB)

No mere army, no looming wall of stone could dampen this man's confidence. His eyes were upon the Lord, and he believed in the God of the impossible.

Let those who are struggling know that wounds are a poor

excuse for abandoning objectives and dreams. Yes, certain goals may need to be adjusted and timetables may need to be expanded, but wounds need not be a road to failure or second best. Ironically, it is often our very wounds themselves that give us a greater drive to aim higher than those without the hurt.

So show your success.

Then challenge and coach others to turn their dreams into reality.

With these seven elements, we can all boldly tell our stories and impact the lives of all who hear. Moses tells the people of Israel: "Remember how the LORD your God led you through the wilderness for forty years, humbling you and testing you to prove your character" (Deuteronomy 8:2, NLT).

We all have a wonderful story, though it may have its moments of pain, sorrow, struggle, anger, guilt, grief, confusion, and desperation. We must let our story be told; we must shout it from the rooftops and let it echo throughout our community. We must tell our friends and children. We must speak about it at home, at work, and wherever we go. We must never let our story be wasted.

A Crisis in Ecuador

Feared for their ferocious cannibal ways, the primitive Auca Indians lived deep in the rainforests of Ecuador. Yet a small band of young missionaries determined in their hearts to share God's love with them.

On January 8, 1956, after several contacts with the

Aucas, Jim Elliot and four other missionaries landed their plane on a short strip of white sand along the Curaray River. Elisabeth Elliot and several other wives waited near a short wave radio to hear how the meeting with the Indians went.

Jim promised to check in by four-thirty, but by five there still was no word from the men. This was not like Jim. As the hours passed, she realized that something must have gone terribly wrong.

During the next few days, Elisabeth learned the details of how her twenty-eight-year-old husband and those with him had been brutally murdered as they offered friendship and love to the natives.

Elisabeth was in shock. *How could this have happened? Why didn't God protect these men? Why would God take such courageous and committed men?* Elisabeth worked through her pain by telling her story and the story of those who had sacrificed their lives.

241

The following year, Elisabeth shared her story with the world in *Through Gates of Splendor.* The writing was healing to her and deeply moved those who read it. As she continued to explore her wounds and experienced God's comfort, she wrote other books, including *Shadow of the Almighty, A Path Through Suffering,* and *The Path of Loneliness.*

By openly telling her story, Elisabeth Elliot has impacted millions of people. Her message of hope and encouragement can be summarized in her own words: "I can honestly say that out of the deepest pain has come the strongest conviction of the presence of God and the love of God."

1. What keeps you from telling your story?

embarrassment	fear of rejection
shame	guilt
exhaustion	pride

2. What is the hardest thing to accept about your story? Why?

3. How can you use your story to serve or help others in dark places?

4. Take some time to write out your story using the seven questions on page 234. Find a good friend and read your story to them.

Moving Forward

[Steve]

I will go anywhere as long as it is forward.

DAVID LIVINGSTONE

ife is an amazing adventure, full of excitement and discouragement, sweet dreams and wicked nightmares, smooth waters and turbulent storms. We wish that all would be bright, people would always be kind, and wounds would fade from our thoughts like an old fairy tale.

Yet this is not reality.

And in all probability, it wouldn't even be healthy.

Maybe we need some pain.

Ann Bradstreet suggests: "If we had no winter, the spring would not be so pleasant." I know that when my wife Tami is gone with girlfriends to the beach for a weekend, I appreciate her more when she returns.

Hurts and hurdles surround us. We resent them and fight against them.

But what if wounds are a means of moving us forward?

What if pain is a teacher and difficulties are opportunities? What if a life without struggle is a wasted life?

When Pope John Paul II was shot by a Turkish assassin, he saw the situation as a chance to model forgiveness. On the one-year anniversary of this attempted murder he said: "In the designs of Providence there are no mere coincidences."

A wound may be a blessed event, if only we embrace the blessing and don't get stuck in the agony and distress of it. We are not minimizing the suffering; we're only saying that it may have a meaning that shines through the darkness. Difficult as it may be right now for you to affirm this, the pain may be worth it.

244

Troubles happen, but life moves on. We either move forward with it or we relive it, focusing over and over again on our difficulty. We all must ask ourselves: *Are we living life in our rearview mirror or with our eyes intently focused on the road ahead?*

Focusing only on the past blocks us from growing. It stunts our growth and entangles us in the most negative emotions of our past. Everything stops. The apostle Paul writes: "One thing I do: Forgetting what is behind and straining toward what is ahead, I press on toward the goal to win the prize for which God has called me heavenward in Christ Jesus" (Philippians 3:13–14).

We all need to push forward, for that is where *life* is. We must start by stepping out.

Stepping Out

"My dream," said ten-year-old Lydia, whose father had died suddenly, "is that next year will be better than this year."

That's what stepping out is all about. It's expecting something better rather than letting anxiety hold you back. Bill and Gloria Gaither summed it up when they wrote: "Because He lives, I can face tomorrow."

Christ gives us strength and comfort and hope. Regardless of the past, He will be with us as we move forward. As Scripture tells us: He was "a man of sorrows, acquainted with bitterest grief" (Isaiah 53:3, NLT).

Jesus understands pain. He suffered so we could be healed and forgiven. He paved a way so we could have a bright tomorrow.

245

FOR US...JESUS WAS...

> despised
> rejected
> weighed down
> wounded
> crushed
> beaten
> whipped
> oppressed
> treated harshly (Isaiah 53:3-7, NLT)

God has great dreams for us; all we need to do is step out and grasp them. We are all bigger than our wounds—

and maybe even bigger *because* of our wounds. Paul wrote to the church at Galatia: "Christ has set us free to live a free life. So take your stand! Never again let anyone put a harness of slavery on you" (Galatians 5:1, *The Message*).

What wonderful counsel! God has set us free—free from our wounds, our guilt, our fears, and our past. We can move forward with confidence and enthusiasm, confident that God is with us and enthusiastic that He has marvelous plans in store for us. Somebody once said: "The shadow will always be behind you if you walk toward the light." Walking toward the light means stepping out and not letting anything stop us. God is waiting for us; all we need is the courage and faith to join Him.

Our future will not be perfect. There will be new challenges, new difficulties, and, yes, new wounds. But we will be stronger for what we have gone through. Louisa May Alcott wrote: "I am not afraid of storms, for I am learning how to sail my ship."

It's interesting that she didn't say that she had *learned* to sail, but that she was *learning*. We are all in process—none of us have arrived. Yet on this journey, with God's help and our determination, we move forward and discover victory.

Emily Main, one of our reviewers, wrote: "We may be wounded for a season or seasons. The beautiful thing about God is that once we allow Him to heal our heart, there is no turning back. Our lives are changed, affecting all our tomorrows. Our wounds are not passed on to the next generation, for the cycle is broken. This is His victory."

Thanking God

It is initially difficult to thank God for our struggles and pain. We want to get angry and ask Him "Why?"

He may answer that "why" question.

He does sometimes.

But not very often.

There are other questions He is much more likely to answer…

What…what is this all about, Lord? What do You want me to learn, to see, to do?

How…how am I to endure this? How will I make it through? How will I get through these dark waters without drowning? How do You want to use this in my life?

But when it comes to questions such as *when* or *why*, we probably shouldn't expect a definitive answer. The "whens" of life are in His hands (Psalm 31:15). And we may never know "why"—at least not until we pass beyond this fragile life and see our Maker face-to-face. Maybe it's important that we don't know all the details about the "whys" of our suffering, for then there would be no need for faith. It is in trusting God through the easy and the difficult that we grow close to Him. And the closer we draw to Him, the easier it is to thank Him for all things.

Gratitude reshapes our attitude, making even the tough times positive. In his book, *Now That I Have Cancer, I Am Whole*, John Robert McFarland writes: "I'm so grateful I never have bad days. I have nauseated days and frightened days. Tired days and hurting days. Long days and short days. Silent days and alone days.... Cold days and warm days. But no bad days. I'm so grateful."

Thankfulness keeps us focused on the positive. It reminds us that there is always hope, and that difficulties will pass. Wounds have their limits, but thankfulness doesn't. In fact, the greater our gratitude, the more we become aware of our healing and that Jesus is truly the ultimate physician.

Gratitude is faith in action. Every moment of every day is full of things for which to be thankful. Randy Stonehill writes: "Celebrate this heartbeat." Gratitude makes us more alive, more enthusiastic, more optimistic. Gratitude is a prism which adds bright colors and twinkling lights to everything we see. In our darkest nights, it is a beacon that guides us to our Heavenly Father.

As Dr. Gregory Jantz writes: "Finding God-given blessings in every hour of distress is one of the most important keys to bouncing back, being resilient, and becoming strong again."

There are millions of things to thank God for; we are only limited by our poor attention, narrow perspective, and lack of faith.

David marveled as he pondered God's goodness and care, writing: "How precious it is, Lord, to realize that you are thinking about me constantly! I can't even count how many times a day your thoughts turn towards me. And when I waken in the morning, you are still thinking of me!" (Psalm 139:17–18, TLB).

Yet as we journey through times of trouble, there are

two things in particular we need to thank Him for.

First, there are *our wounds* themselves.

They are gifts, while at the same time being tests. As Helen Keller wrote: "I thank God for my handicaps for, through them, I have found myself, my work, and my God."

Second, there is *God's presence.*

He is always right beside us, even when we don't feel His arm around our shoulders. The prophet Isaiah recognizes God's role as "a refuge for the needy in his distress, a shelter from the storm and a shade from the heat" (Isaiah 25:4). He has been these things for each one of us, and we need to thank Him. Not because He needs our gratitude, but because we need to give it. Thanking God makes all things worthwhile.

Embracing Eternity

This life is not all there is. At its very best, in the sweetest and most sublime of moments, it is only a brief glimpse at a unimaginably beautiful world beyond our physical senses. This life is shorter than we realize, but eternity is longer than we can imagine. Randy Alcorn, founder of Eternal Perspective Ministries, pictures our life as a small dot on an infinite line. Moses writes, "Seventy years are given to us! Some may even reach eighty. But even the best of these years are filled with pain and trouble; soon they disappear, and we are gone" (Psalm 90:10, NLT).

That is when our real life begins.

What we currently experience is simply a foretaste, a warm-up, a shadow, a prologue to the real thing. Beyond this life is a land called heaven which has no tears, no troubles, no suffering, no wounds. It is a world where everything is healed and nothing is broken. This is the land where we belong. As Abraham Lincoln said: "Man was made for immortality."

Our wounds make us more willing to let go of what we have here. Our trials and troubles cause us to look forward to a better, more glorious world. Peter explains that "we are looking forward to the new heavens and new earth he has promised" (2 Peter 3:13, NLT).

Our sufferings and struggles make us impatient for an eternity unmarred by the painful realities we face daily. Francis DeSales wrote: "We will soon be in eternity, and then we will see how all the affairs of the world are such little things."

Living in the light of eternity places everything in perspective. It gives our days new meaning and causes us to reprioritize what matters most. Eternity points out our foolishness and plants a peace in our heart that defies current circumstances. Looking forward *draws* us forward. It constantly reminds us that Matthew Henry was right when he said: "It ought to be the business of every day to prepare for our last day." But let me add to this: "and all the days of eternity."

Life is full of challenges! Why this fact surprises so many people is baffling. Sure, some people appear to have light challenges while others have seemingly overwhelming challenges. As Rick Warren writes: "Life on earth is a test." Each and every difficulty is a test to determine our patience, courage, character, determination, and faith. Sometimes we handle our challenges well, sometimes we don't. The apostle James reminds us that "God blesses the people who patiently endure testing. Afterward they will receive the crown of life that God has promised to those who love him" (James 1:12, NLT).

As we each learn how to deal with our wounds, our perspective on this world improves and our appreciation of the next increases. In heaven, we will gain incomprehensibly amazing rewards based on how we pass the tests in this life. Yet, because of God's grace, even if we don't pass the tests, eternity will still be full of joy, radiance, and transcendent beauty. As D. L. Moody said: "Take courage. We walk in the wilderness today and the Promised Land tomorrow."

Unquenchable Faith

We all wish life were a playground, but the Bible tells us it's a battleground. We get tackled, beat up, and wounded. Yet through it all, our faith grows. And as our faith grows, we draw closer and closer to God.

Paul tells us, "In every battle you will need faith as your shield" (Ephesians 6:16, NLT). Several years later he wrote: "Endure hardship with us like a good soldier" (2 Timothy 2:3). On the battlegrounds of life, our faith has the potential to grow stronger and deeper. Our wounds become symbols of our fight. They are nothing for which to feel ashamed or insecure. In God's eyes there is nothing wrong with our wounds.

Difficulties are opportunities to move forward. They can bring out the best or the worst in us, depending on how we see them and what we do with them. Troubles transform us, if we let them. As we've said before: Challenges can be what empower us and take us to the next level. God doesn't want to hurt us, but He is willing to use our pain to accomplish great things in us and around us. Zane Grey once wrote that his recipe for greatness was "to bear up under loss, to fight the bitterness of defeat and the weakness of grief, to be a victor over anger, to smile when tears are close…to look up with unquenchable faith in something ever more about to be."

This is what I want: an unquenchable faith.

Yet without wounds, my faith remains untested. And without moving forward, my faith will be unrewarded.

In the end, we must never forget that God loves us. He yearns to heal our wounds when the time is right. He is waiting to comfort us as soon as we ask Him. He is eager to strengthen us as we lean more and more on Him.

So as we walk this trouble-filled world, let us hold firmly to His joy, His peace, His purpose, and especially His hope. For it is through hope that we move forward, and it is in moving forward that we discover that God can meet our every need.

1. What ideas in this book have most helped you move forward? What story did you most identify with? How have you progressed in your healing?

2. Gratitude makes us more alive, more enthusiastic, more optimistic. How has this proven true in your life?

3. When you think of your wounds in light of eternity, what new perspectives come to mind?

4. List three ideas from this book that have been most helpful to you. Take some time to meet with another who is suffering, and encourage him or her with these concepts.

Questions for Group Discussion

Prologue: The Dark Night

1. How have people responded to your speaking about your wounds in the past?

2. What fears do you have about openly sharing your wounds?

3. How do you hope people in this group will respond as you open up about your deep hurts?

Chapter One: Too Much Rain

1. Choose any three of the following questions and tell your answers to your group:

   a. Which wounds most need my attention?

   b. How are my wounds affecting me today?

   c. Where am I on the path of healing?

    d. How can my wounds make me a stronger person?

    e. How can God use my wounds for good?

2. How do you feel when good-hearted people give you pat answers or simplistic formulas to deal with your pain? When has this happened to you? How did you deal with it?

3. How have other people in your life given you hope?

Chapter Two: Lampposts in the Dark

1. Speak about a time when your pain has confused you. Frequently confusion occurs when we are feeling two or more emotions at the same time. What combined emotions create the most confusion in you? (e.g., love and hate, anger and sadness, grief and relief, fear and excitement)

2. We have made the statement: "Feeling is healing." How does this statement strike you? Is it easy or difficult for you to connect with this idea? Why?

3. Read 2 Corinthians 4:6–9. Circle the words or phrases that most touch your heart. Tell your group why you most identify with those particular words.

Chapter Three: Good Grief

1. Is it hard or easy for you to lean on others when you are grieving? Why?

2. Describe a time in your life when you needed to lean on others. How did they support you?

3. Of the eight suggestions offered on page 55 under "How to Help Me As I Grieve," which three do you need the most?

Chapter Four: Hidden Faces

1. Why are guilt and shame so devastating to people?

2. Read John 8:1–11, the story of the woman caught in adultery. With which characters in this story do you most identify: the woman caught, the guy that got away, those holding the stones, or Jesus offering forgiveness?

3. Of the ten "Shame's Talk" statements on page 76, which are you most likely to say to yourself? What is your reaction to God's answer, as found next to those shame statements?

Chapter Five: Facing Fears and Finding Peace

1. What frightened you most when you were a child? (The dark, spiders or snakes, rejection, failure, heights, anger, death, loss of parents, _____.) Are any of these fears still present today?

2. F-E-A-R = False Evidence Appearing Real. Describe a time in your life when that happened. How did you react? Who came alongside you and offered you some objectivity?

3. When have you experienced God's peace? Describe what it feels like. Share what enabled you to experience His peace.

Chapter Six: Letting Go of Anger

1. What typically triggers anger in you?

2. How do your wounds make you more vulnerable to anger? What self-talk about your wounds keeps angry flames burning?

3. Which of the Cool Words on page 101 could turn the heat down on your anger this week? Share them with your group.

Chapter Seven: The Art of Overcoming

1. What hurts from your past have you already released? What healing have you experienced from this? What helped you let go?

2. What hurts in your past are the most difficult to release? Please explain.

3. Who is the most optimistic person you know? How does his or her optimism affect you? Which of the following characteristics of optimism would you like to incorporate more of into your life? (Refer to pages 120–122—see the best, believe the best, choose the best, live the best.)

259

Chapter Eight: Darkness and Land Mines

1. See the acrostic C-O-M-P-A-R-E on page 128. In which of these ways are you tempted to compare yourself with others?

2. When are you most likely to complain? How does complaining make you feel?

3. Identify three positive qualities about each member in your group. Speak about these qualities around the circle.

Chapter Nine: Embraced by God's Healing Presence

1. Speak about a time when you called on God and...

   - He seemed silent

   - you felt worse

   - He gave you peace

   - He gave you direction

   - you heard His voice

   - you sensed His presence

2. When has God ever physically, emotionally, or spiritually rescued you?

3. How has your faith helped you heal?

Chapter Ten: The Comfort of Caring People

1. What do you need most from others when you are in pain? Their words, their touch, or their presence? Why?

2. Which of the eight ideas listed in "How to Connect with Others" on page 163 would be the easiest for you to apply this week?

3. How would a coach be helpful to you at this time in your life? Of the traits listed on page 167, in which areas would you like help?

Chapter Eleven: Triumph from Tragedy

1. "Pain makes man think." How has this been true in your life?

2. Give an example of a time when adversity enriched your life. Have you grown in terms of maturity, courage, compassion, character, faith?

3. Who has been the greatest model of triumph over tragedy for you?

Chapter Twelve: Fresh New Beginnings

1. What do the following words of the Lord mean to you at this time in your life? "If you return to me, I will restore you.... I will give you back your health and heal your wounds" (Jeremiah 15:19; 30:17, NLT). How do you need God to make this promise real to you today?

2. List three ways that you can create a fresh start for yourself tomorrow morning. What are the potential obstacles you may encounter?

3. Jesus came to fill your pain with His presence. How do you experience Him in the midst of your pain? If you don't experience Him, what could you do to open the door to Him?

261

Chapter Thirteen: Trusting Again

1. Why is it so hard to trust? When is it the easiest for you to trust, and why?

2. Which of the items under "Things to Let Go Of" on page 204 do you need to release?

3. What risk would you take if you were guaranteed not to fail? What would be your first step? When could you take this first step?

Chapter Fourteen: Please Be Kind to You

1. When is the last time you took a break? What do you do to recharge your batteries?

2. How many hours of sleep do you allow yourself each night? How many hours do you really need? What can you do to better meet your sleep needs?

3. What style of music relaxes you the most? Tell your group the name of your favorite relaxing CD.

Chapter Fifteen: Tell Your Story

1. Make a list of three low points in your life, and relate one of them to your group.

2. Which of the "Seven S's" on pages 236–240 come the most naturally to you?

3. With whom have you felt safest telling your story? What elements of your story might help others in pain?

Chapter Sixteen: Moving Forward

1. We make the statement, "We are bigger than our wounds—and maybe even bigger *because* of our wounds." Has this been your experience?

2. Are you ready to move forward? What is stopping you and what is helping you?

3. Life becomes sweeter as we enthusiastically embrace our future. For which of the following things do you need to ask God to help you do that: Wisdom, strength, confidence, friendships, protection, courage, forgiveness, hope?

Notes

1. Portions of these five steps have been previously published in *The Worn Out Woman* by Steve Stephens and Alice Gray (Sisters, OR: Multnomah, 2004), 157–164.
2. Stormie Omartian, *Stormie: A Story of Forgiveness and Healing* (Eugene, OR: Harvest House Publishers, 1997).
3. Amy Harmon, "Sad, Lonely World Discovered in Cyberspace," *The New York Times*, August 30, 1998.

Are you even thinking about walking out?

"I'm at the point where I don't think it is worth the effort anymore."

"The only reason I'm staying is because of the children."

"Surely God doesn't want me to be this unhappy."

Every woman longs to be appreciated, valued, and cared for. When these needs go unmet, she may be tempted to leave the husband she once loved—but walking out is seldom the path to happiness.

Like trusted friends, Dr. Steve Stephens and Alice Gray offer wise and gentle advice to restore hope to your marriage. You'll discover proven methods for how you can move toward each other rather than away, build up instead of tear down, and find love rather than lose it.

1-59052-267-2

the walk out woman

Dr. Steve Stephens Alice Gray

Also from
PAM VREDEVELT

Life-Changing Advice in a Quick-to-Read Format!

With sales of over 700,000 copies, the Lists to Live By series has something for everyone—guidance, inspiration, humor, family, love, health, and home. These books are perfect gift books for all occasions.